DIARY OF THE D.C. SNIPER

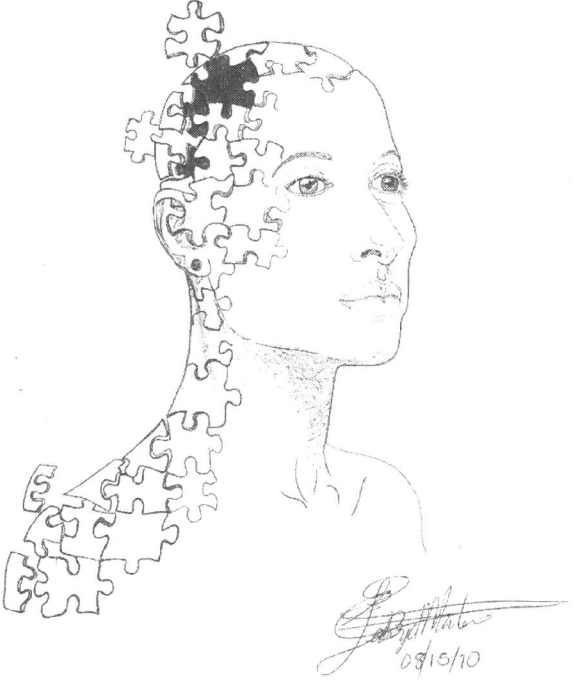

WRITTEN AND AUTHORIZED FOR RELEASE BY
LEE BOYD MALVO
WITH ANTHONY MEOLI, MA, J.D.

U.S. Copyright Information:

Type of Work: Text
Registration Number / Date: TXu001814122 / 2012-06-27
Application Title: The Diary of the D.C. Sniper.
Title: The Diary of the D.C. Sniper.
Copyright Claimant: Anthony Meoli, 1970- , Transfer: By written
agreement.
Date of Creation: 2012
Authorship on Application: Anthony Meoli, 1970- ; Citizenship:
United States. Authorship: text of introduction and conclusion,
compilation, editing.
Lee Malvo; Domicile: United States; Citizenship: United States.
Authorship: text, Lee Malvo provided his hand-written memoir,
original art and original poetry.
Copyright Note: C.O. correspondence.
Names: Meoli, Anthony, 1970-Malvo, Lee

Written by: Lee Boyd Malvo
Contributor, Author and Editor: Anthony Meoli
All Illustrations and Cover Artwork: Lee Boyd Malvo
Cover & Jacket Design: Anthony Meoli

Third Printing: July 24, 2014

10 9 8 7 6 5 4 3

DIARY OF THE D.C. SNIPER

This book is dedicated to the victims, families and all of those who

were traumatized by the D.C. Sniper shootings in October 2002.

The diary contains very disturbing and mature content, therefore it is

not intended for young readers.

Lee Boyd Malvo will not profit from the sale

of this book.

30% of the net proceeds will be donated to charity.

Acknowledgements

To my wife and daughter.

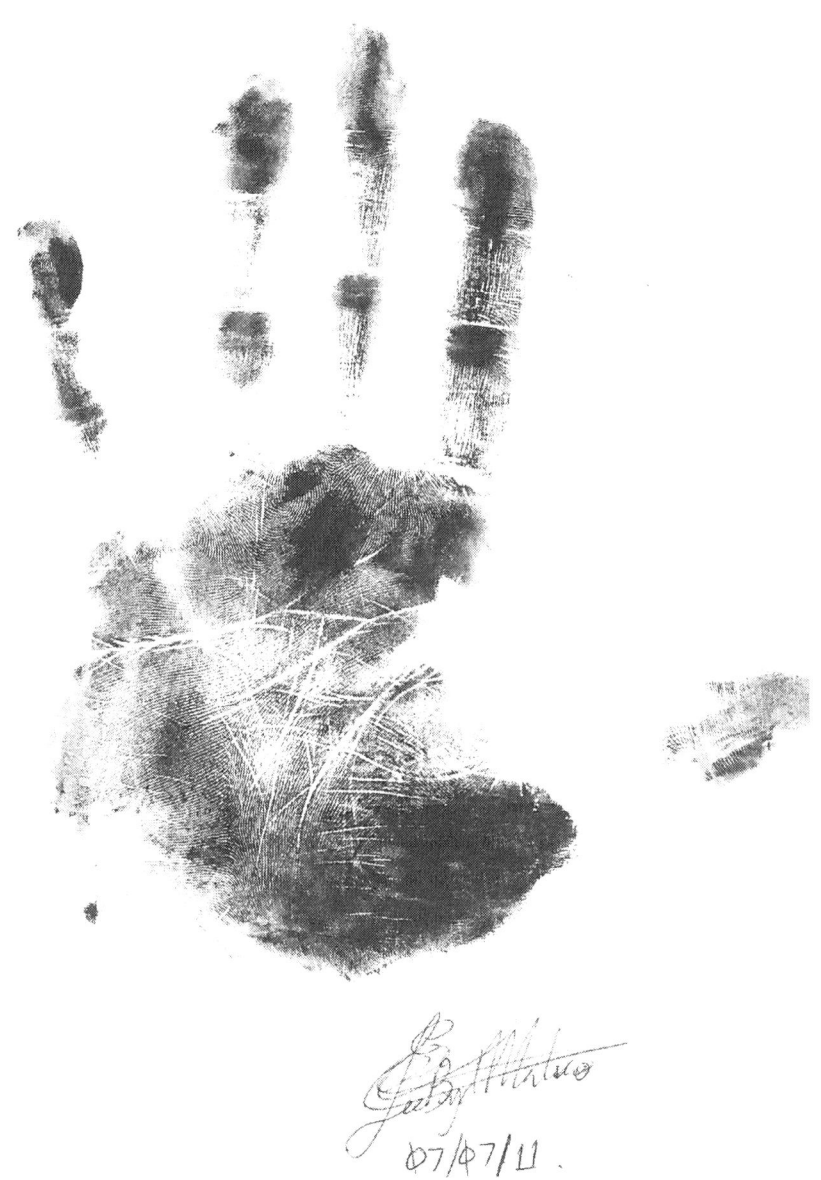

Actual Handprint of Lee Boyd Malvo

"Ms. James, the child needs a stable home somewhere to settle down; he cannot keep rolling from place to place. This is doing him no good. You have an intelligent son who can do well if he has a steady support system."

- Former Guidance Counselor of Lee Boyd Malvo

"If you dance with the Devil long enough, eventually you become his partner."

- Anthony Meoli

About the Co-Author, Anthony Meoli

Education

➢ *B.S. – Administration of Justice – Penn State University*
➢ *M.A. – Forensic Psychology – Argosy University*
➢ *J.D. – John Marshall Law School*

Professional Experience

Anthony Meoli has personally spoken with numerous serial/spree killers and death row inmates including: Danny Rolling, Richard Ramirez, Glen Edward Rogers, Loran Cole, Kenneth Bianchi, Isaac Zamora, Elmer Wayne Henley and Lee Boyd Malvo.

Anthony appeared as a criminal profiler in the documentary "My Brother the Serial Killer." His television appearances include CBS affiliate WRDW in Augusta, GA and ID Discovery. He has been a guest on over 25 radio stations speaking about serial personalities and the many factors and traumatic events that often lead towards violence.

He has recorded two audio CD interviews with Lee Boyd Malvo (*Interview with the D.C. Sniper*) and Isaac L. Zamora (*I Kill for God*), a spree shooter in Washington State. Both audio CD's were made available so that educators and the general public can understand the exact events and motives in the inmate's own words.

Anthony Meoli is a certified forensic consultant with the ACFEI (American College of Forensic Examiners Institute) and currently sits on the Consulting Committee with the AISOCC (American International Society of Cold Cases). His articles have appeared in the Forensic Examiner and Psychology Today.

Written Correspondence

For over sixteen years Mr. Meoli has written to over one-hundred serial killers, both domestically and abroad. Some of these men and women have maintained steady correspondence for nearly a decade.

He has written steadily to Lee Boyd Malvo since 2005. It was through this exchange of hundreds of letters and numerous telephone calls that Lee's confidence and trust were earned. This unique relationship provided the basis for the release of this once private information.

Table of Contents

Introduction – Obtaining the Diary

My initial interest in writing Lee Boyd Malvo in 2005 stemmed from approximately seven years of previously writing and visiting death row inmates. My goal, as it always has been, was to explore inmates as individuals, and as human beings. Regardless of their crimes or charges levied against them, the basic notion was that I could learn more about them or the rationale behind their crimes if I simply connected with them on a more intimate and psychological level. In Lee's particular case, I had no idea that my first letter would eventually begin the process of allowing him to provide the information that you are about to read.

Due to the various jurisdictions in which the shootings occurred coupled with Lee constantly moving from one undisclosed facility to another, most of my initial attempts at contacting him were returned undelivered. This was largely due to the increased security required by the Department of Corrections which had essentially banned Malvo's ability to receive mail or speak to the outside world.

Lee's first written response was received on February 6, 2005. He was very hesitant at responding to my initial attempts to contact him. Upon receiving a response he began by writing, "I am intrigued by your candor and I will extend to you much of the same." He went on, "Currently, you are the only person with whom I correspond, I hate games and I am rather blunt. I am not known to mince my words. I am a black and white kind of guy; but you are either for or against me." I knew that it would be a challenge getting to know Lee's multi-faceted personality, but I slowly began my journey.

Over the next few months we wrote quite often. At the time I was living in New Orleans Louisiana and Hurricane Katrina had not only taken part of my home, but with it much of my time. However, whenever possible, I continued to write. Lee would always respond within a few weeks' time. We lost touch after I was forced to move from Louisiana in 2007 due to a job change, but we began anew once I resettled.

In early 2008, I began writing Lee much more often, wanting to learn more about him and his childhood. There were several issues within his letters that I found compelling about his childhood that seemed to have gone unresolved. I was also surprised, given the gravity of the crimes that had taken place; there were no authorized books written about his life. It became my goal to find out exactly who Lee Boyd Malvo was, where he grew up, what his family life was like and how he came to meet John Allen Muhammad. Arguably, the question that plagued me the most was how an individual who was of at least average intelligence, very well read, well-spoken (over the phone), could have possibly been influenced by another person to the point of becoming complicit in such devastatingly tragic and seemingly random crimes.

Lee had been made aware of my formal background in criminal justice and law from my very first letter. However, during the final two years before he decided to release his diary, I informed him of my acceptance into a Master's of Arts in Forensic Psychology at Argosy University in Atlanta, Georgia. After five years of writing, he trusted that I was truly interested in learning more about what had triggered his "anger response," as I would eventually call it – and what I would find out was astounding.

While enrolled in the Master's program, I spoke to Lee on a monthly basis. Although the calls were often difficult to coordinate, we finally worked out a system that allowed for fielding his calls on a more routine basis. Soon we were talking two to three times every month. Considering that Lee Boyd Malvo is only allowed about four (20 minute) telephone calls per month, taking three consecutive calls required a great deal of trust on his part. These calls were more than half of his allotted human interaction for the entire month.

Although I was certainly not acting as Lee's therapist, my growing education in forensic psychology helped begin the process of finding answers to some my questions, which often crossed the line of comfort for Lee. As time progressed, Lee's natural defenses dropped and he began to share information that was more personal with each successive call. Over time, I earned his confidence.

My interest concerned how his childhood shaped who he would become later in life. The artwork and poetry he would often include with his letters showed a great deal of pain and psychological trauma. It was as if Lee had spent his entire life in some state of turmoil. Lee was searching for something to hold onto, someone to trust, but they never came.

His calls continued to come. Lee had decided that it was finally time to cleanse his mind by telling his life's story. Lee revealed his intentions in letters in the latter part of 2009 and on the phone in early 2010. What he admitted was that there existed a hand-written memoir or "diary" which he had written two years after the shootings occurred. This "diary" was a personal reflection of the many events, traumas and actions that Lee had experienced and been exposed to throughout his life.

It took a few more months to convince Lee that along with his diary, his original poetry and artwork would help to better explain his account of these crimes. The poetry and artwork were completed at various times during Lee's 10 years of incarceration and provide unique insight into how he saw the events unfold at that particular moment in time.

The diary arrived as a 175-page hand-written document on May 9, 2011. It was transcribed verbatim with only minimal alterations when necessary. These changes were worked out during numerous phone calls in order to protect the names of friends, family members and victims.

This book's sole intention is to explore and explain why these crimes occurred. It is fully authorized by Lee Boyd Malvo and the only book containing his entire diary, original artwork and poetry.

Anthony Meoli, MA, J.D.

The Setup

We were parked in a very large parking lot of a shopping center in Montgomery County Maryland or somewhere around this area. The Chevy Caprice was nestled between three cars. The trunk of the car was in a direct line of sight with the front door and parking lot of a Michael's craft store.

The first order of business was to plot out the routes of the immediate vicinity (once the shot had been taken). Muhammad and I sat before a laptop to decide which of the four routes presented the least traffic, was the shortest to our next destination, and so on. Once we had selected the route and its' alternate, Muhammad popped the trunk.

Held fast by bungee cords, the trunk was opened about two inches. Muhammad lowered the seat and slid over into the back. The backrest of the backseat was hinged on two hooks, of which he simply lifted off to access the trunk. The bracing for the backrest had now been removed.

First, he positioned the back rest and spare tire in the trunk. The spare tire was used as a hand rest when shooting. Having positioned these items, Muhammad then assembled the AR-15.

We would spend roughly two to three weeks of reconnaissance before settling on an area to strike. While Muhammad got settled in the trunk, it was my job to ensure that no one happened to be sitting in the cars around us or loitering nearby.

The inside of the trunk was painted the exact same shade of dark blue as the car itself. A passerby would have had to be keenly observant to notice. A *3"x2"* incision was made, cut into the trunk right under and adjacent to the key lock. This provided a total of five inches which was sufficient space. The rifle stayed within the enclosure of the car, which acted as a natural suppressor to muffle the sound. Muhammad would always be in the center so all he had to do was swivel a little, left or right, to select a "target." The entire setup was derived from an Irish Republican Army manual. Muhammad simply modified it.

"Do I have a go?" Muhammad asked. "No." I replied. A man a few cars down was unpacking items into his minivan. Once the man had left I gave him the "all clear."

When I gave the go ahead, immediately a shot rang out. The bullet punched a hole into the glass at the front of the Michael's craft store. Muhammad had missed. The young man he was aiming for was hopping, causing Muhammad to either pull up or mistimed the shot.

The fact that he had missed was never discussed. He returned from the trunk and slid back into the driver's seat and followed the directions on the map. I then hopped over into the backseat and placed the backrest back upon the hooks. Next I disassembled the AR-15 and placed it back into its bag. That was the *first* shot. Before going to bed Muhammad said; "There will be no more missed opportunities!"

Lee Boyd Malvo

Chapter 1: The Separation

I was born on February 18, 1985 to Una James, my mother, age 21 and to Leslie Malvo, my father, age 37 in Kingston, Jamaica. My father was a mason by trade, a quiet man in most respects, he was not fond of arguing, and he was also the most emotionally available adult in the family.

When my father was home, I was with him, doing whatever he did, which is not all that uncommon for boys. My father had no preconceived notions or hidden agendas as to who I should be – he just loved and accepted me. So simple this was for he was a simple unlettered man with simple tastes. I would spend the next twelve years after the separation of my parents searching for this simple acceptance. But I am getting ahead of myself. In those five years, my father administered corporal punishment once; it was done within limits unlike the abuse I would come to know quite intimately at the hands of my mother.

Most of my time with "Brown Man," as my father was known, was spent on a tricycle. Before I learned to pedal he would tie a rope around the handlebars and pull me to and fro wherever we went. In some cases, I would hitch a ride on his shoulders. In fact, upon those shoulders is where I had my first epiphany.

I must have been around three years of age at the time, we were in the ice cream parlor and my ice cream fell off the cone. My father simply just purchased another ice cream. I recall examining the entire package, my dad looking up at me. I then had the "a-ha moment." I bit the cone at the bottom and with a little suction and funneled out the ice cream downward. The memory stands out because of my father's reaction – he told everyone!

I was a little caramel complexioned replica of him, his pride and joy. I remember two incidents in which my father came to my rescue. The first, he arrived from work, he was on the veranda with is tool bag. I immediately ran behind him to escape the blows of my mother I would receive for playing with the other kids in the tenement yard.

He picked me up with his rough hands and gently wiped away my tears. I pointed at the other children romping in the dirt as if to say that was our playground, and he understood. He glared at my mother as he knew what she was doing. My mother replied, "He does not listen." My father countered stating, "You have to release the boy to go play sometimes – can't have him pent up in the house-all day!" "Well, he won't, not until he reads this book." said my mother. So, this is where I found myself, between the polar opposites of my parents.

Many of my earlier memories are similar to the above incident. The second such incident that stands out for me is as follows. Since the age of two, I was obsessed with planes, my dad knew that I wanted to fly; he understood my three years' old speech. Anyhow, I was a plane, arms outstretched, concentrating on my motions as I maneuvered around the obstacles of the furniture. My dad happened to be house-cleaning and cooking. I was not allowed in the kitchen while he cooked so I was occupying myself in my own adventure. He must have heard all the commotion. First, the vase hitting the floor and then the peeling voice of my mother, *"LEEEEEE!"*

I stood frozen before my handiwork. I had thought to myself, "Wasn't I warned to stay out of the living room away from the crockery?" Again, I found myself between both parents. I was sobbing, looking from one to the other. My Mother went off and she grabbed me by one hand and began to spank me, my father wrestled me away from her grasp. I will never forget what he said. He bent down and grabbed a shard from the broken vase and he held it right before my face and handed it to my mother. "Una," he said, "this is a person – that is a thing – one can be replaced – the other cannot." He repeated that first part, "This is a person." (Pointing at me) and "that is a thing" (Pointing at the shards of broken porcelain) while looking at my mother. "One can be replaced, the other cannot!"

When I was four years of age my father was granted a permit to work in Grand Cayman. The rate of currency exchange was in favor of the Cayman dollar, it was a good opportunity to earn some money to finally get an hour of our own – and out of the tenement, out of the ghetto.

Turning to my mother, we must reasonably examine her make-up. All plans were created by my mother, buying a house, saving, returning to school - she was an upwardly mobile, driven, disciplinarian. My father was no saint either, he was a man-whore and philanderer and he had a gambling addiction: dominoes and horses.

Every fortnight my father would have to deliver "x amount" of dollars to my mother for all the bills, savings, and to cover the cost of her tuition (She was learning the trade of a seamstress and wanted to be a fashion designer). On this one weekend, my father was short, so my mother arrived at the conclusion that he had given the money to his other women (being that he had been caught red-handed in the act before – she was within reason to assume this). They got in to an argument and my father knocked one or two of my mother's teeth out. This was one beating too many.

Every Sunday my father would clean the house along with every other chore plus cooking. One day while my father was cleaning, I watched as he dusted off the dresser. While cleaning the mirror he catches a glimpse of my mother through the reflection as she makes her way toward him bearing a machete in her upraised hand. My father reacted too little, too late. Although her attempt to cut off his hand failed, she succeeded at slicing off the thumb of his right hand. My dad retrieved the digit, stitched and bandaged it. My mother abandoned me, him and the house for a month after the incident – so he would know what it felt like to live in her shoes. You know it worked. Never again did my father raise his hands against my mother.

For several months I would share the violent machete event with strangers on the bus and wherever else; "Want to know a secret?" and when they obliged I replied aloud "Mommy tried to kill Daddy!" I would get slapped on the mouth and my mother would apologetically try to explain away my comments. I was a chatterbox - she told everyone. What irked her the most was how I phrased the subject, "Mommy tried to kill Daddy," as if she was somehow to blame. My mother had a very bad temper and when it flared she would beat me savagely, drawing blood – as she too was beaten by her mother.

    My mother and I have an inconsistent relationship to this day. She has always had an agenda, a picture in her head of the "perfect son" and tried but failed to live out some of her dreams vicariously through me. This was a burden that weighed heavily on our relationship. Children do need discipline, but her brand was "beat-downs." She was intolerable of mistakes from anyone but unwilling to ever admit her own errors. When it came to my parents I was simply a possession to one, and a child to the other.

My mother was fanatical when it came to education – my education, she was a perfectionist, good was never good enough. The daily abuse, the verbal tongue-lashing of my worthlessness took a heavy toll. This, coupled with the perfectionism and her unstable attitude, caused me withdraw from her. One moment she was bubbly and the next the complete opposite, becoming irritable and explosive over the smallest things. Is it sane to expect a four year old to fold his clothes perfectly and not make mistakes? I was beaten daily, multiple times with just about anything you could think of – and never did she discriminate where on my body to deliver the punishment.

When she was in a good mood she would teach me how to draw. I was tentative around her and she did not like it, she did not have the patience or the wisdom to understand why I wouldn't speak to her unless absolutely necessary, why I'd seek comfort in sharing my most intimate thoughts with perfect strangers – yet cold to her.

With the extra money my dad had earned from working over six months in the Grand Cayman, we were able to move from Oakland road and out of the tenement to a residential area of Watthom Park. While there, I was enrolled in a private school. Whether or not my mother's tutoring played a part in my ability to thrive at school, I can't say – but academically I was ahead of the pack.

I found a nice balance between my authoritarian mother who would not have me play at all (but have me read, study, and learn to put into my own words by explaining things back to her) and my laid back old man who got a kick out of my silliness and encouraged me to simply be – *me*. A balance was struck, but it teetered on a thin thread that would soon snap.

My mom caught word that my father was living with another woman in Grand Cayman, and severed all ties with him. She emptied the bank accounts and swept the house clean of all his belongings. We left Kingston and moved to the rural Endeavor in the Parish of St. Ann. What first stood out to me about Endeavor were how green it was and the braying of donkeys. This rural district was a long way from the metropolitan atmosphere of Kingston. It was an agrarian society; everyone knew everything about the comings and goings of their neighbors. It was rude not to say good morning or to pass by an elder without inquiring about their welfare.

I enrolled in Brown's Town Basic School. I had one choice – *do well*. My mother and Aunt Marie were partners in a bar and retail shop at this time to help pay for the schooling. Very quickly my mother launched into her "doomed to fail" endeavor to strip any facets of my father that polluted me. First, she berated my father's "ways" with constant remarks of disdain concerning him. I would always defend him no matter how many "ass-whoopings" I received in return. I was as stubborn as she was, every day some new fault in me was to be found, how I was just like my father in this or that way, and how she would get it out of me one way or the other.

All of my toys were replaced with nursery rhyme books among others. Again, I was not allowed to play or interact with the other children. I was always under her watchful eye because I was never going to amount to any good unless my mother made something of me. I was a fairly intelligent child with a photographic memory that I still possess to this day. When I went somewhere I could easily retrace my steps. I learned to place little pit-stops in my memory, things that stood out to me, each one leading to the other – these images were my icons. I was entrusted to travel with Kaman, the oldest son Ms. Donna (a friend of my mother's), who was only 4 at the time while I was around 6 ½ years old. Of course our mothers had everyone between our bus stop and school look out for us for safety reasons. I took a liking to Kaman, as he was very perceptive with an inquisitive and bubbly personality. I enjoyed my responsibility being an only child. Kaman filled a void for me. Ms. Donna was to become a surrogate mother to me, and years later, even, a home away from home.

With the money her and my father had saved, my mother had invested in the business and with the rest purchased a house. With my father out of the picture, she was free to date. A relative of my aunt's husband, Clive, was very much interested in my mother. Clive, in an attempt to win my mother's affection, showered her with gifts – some of which he had already promised to other people such as my aunt and her husband. The sisters had a falling out behind this incident. Since my mother was the one who rented the space and put up the capital to start both of the businesses, my aunt was ousted. My mother was not pleased with Clive for obvious reasons and ended the short fling. She did not return his gifts. This argument between the sisters became the talk of the little agrarian community. Flare ups between my aunt and my mother would continue unabated for months.

Then there was Charles Lawrence. I really disliked this guy; I saw him as a real interloper and treated him as such. Now, I was never outwardly disrespectful, it was more in the form of subtle contempt. "Children are to be seen and not heard" or so goes the dictum. Temper tantrums were a "no-no," that would result in a beat-down, better a silent protest. My mother was really bewitched by this guy. He had no trade, no skills or money and was still living with his parents at the age 27. Even I, as a five and a half year old, (and my aunt who I visited in secret) believed this guy to be a bum. Within a short period of three months Charles went from merely hanging around the shop to sleeping over a few nights a week. Even then I refused to speak to him. I would sit across the table or pass him in the hallway without making eye contact. On the flipside, I didn't respond this way with Clive. Although I can't say that I was really open with him either, but I was willing to give the guy a chance. Charles was sneaky, he had crafty eyes, so said my five-and-a-half year old radar.

One such morning Charles couldn't find his shoes and thought to tease blame my way, naturally he assumed, due to my standoffish "attitude" towards him. He brought his suspicions to the attention of my mother who then accused me of hiding the shoes. She confronted me and not only did I refuse to acknowledge or answer her, I stared her down as well. I looked at her from head to toe. First, she smacked that "look off my face," then got a belt and used the leather end with the buckle to beat me. She hit me everywhere and when it was all said and done I had welts all over my body, and my eye was swollen along with blood pouring from my head. And as if the beating itself wasn't bad enough, the biggest insult to injury was the fact that it all stemmed from this guy. He later claimed to find the shoes behind a chair. I looked at him from across the room and this insidious son-of-a-bitch was smiling at me. Soon he began to administer corporal punishment himself within five months of knowing me. He didn't beat me down but rather pinch me and wring my flesh between his fingers until the skin pilled off. My mother was in love and claimed I was only intent on spoiling her happiness and so she turned a blind eye and deaf ear to my complaints.

I soon started a pattern of passive aggressive behavior in retaliation. I couldn't fight back with blows so instead I broke my mother's most cherished crockery and I began to stay out late. I hated my life; Charles would put me in a corner regularly, pinching and taunting me with every chance he got. He would never do these things in the presence of my mother. He had a key and could come and go as he pleased. To add to my torment I was also being molested by the babysitter, an older woman. I didn't complain to my mother because she wouldn't believe me anyway.

I would increasingly stay out late and after school wait to ride the very last bus home. Look, if I was home early, chances are I'd get punished for something, so why not do something to get punished – hell – it will happen if I do and if I don't. I would hang out with friends at their homes if within a reasonable distance of the school. When their parents questioned me about my parents I would lie. School would let out at around 2pm; however, I wouldn't arrive home until about 7pm.

Both my mother and I were quite stubborn – I'd had found more passive and less brazen ways to get back at her. She figured out that I was doing and automatically attributed my many lies and obstinacies to my father. I lied because the truth, I had come to learn, would only lead to more terrible beatings. Lies seemed to work better with my bipolar mother's violent temper. My acting out didn't involve causing trouble at school or hurting other children – it had a target – I was retaliating while simultaneously hiding from what I deemed a very unstable person – which was my own mother.

My first and last pet was a kitten that I had named, "Charlie." And being a kitten it would defecate and pee wherever and whenever it needed to go. The cat slept with me. At the time, culturally, animals did not live in the house with people, cats in particular. They were deemed suspicious critters often stoned whenever in sight, most of them feral. Charlie was part of a litter of feral cats that lived under the shop where my mother did business. In fact, when she cleaned the deep freezers, she fed them the old meat. I came to care for Charlie because his mother would not care for him, so I stepped in and nursed the neglected kitten back to health. In doing so I became attached. Being an only child and unable to play with my peers, I enjoyed talking to him. It served me well in this regard as it was very therapeutic. I snuck the cat into the house and had him in a box in my closet. My mother was oblivious to him taking residence in our home until she caught wind of urine and feces. To the luck of the kitten I caught her in a good mood and promised to house train and clean up behind him. One day Charlie managed to escape my room and urinated all over the sofa – so naturally my mother decided that he had to go. She flew into a rage so I told her I'd do it – fearing that she'd slam the cat against the wall or ground and kill it. I took him out of the box in my closet as he was sleeping. I sat with him on the steps until he awakened. It was a Saturday morning; and rain had fallen during the night. First, I closed the door as he was trying to get inside, then I pointed and told him to go. He kept rubbing his body against my ankles, walking between my legs over and over again. Next to the steps was a broom that I used to sweep the paved area surrounding the house, I picked up the broom and pushed Charlie off the steps. He thought I was playing and would try to dodge the broom and run to my feet. He was very agile and nimble, making it past the broom again and again. "Lee, get rid of the damn cat and come in here and eat your breakfast, it's getting cold!" Now, how my mother stressed the "E" in my name meant different things – when the long "E" ended with a grunt, mom was agitated, moments from tearing into my ass. I swatted Charlie with the broom, but that did not work. I grabbed the back of his neck as he tried to return up the steps, walking him out to the driveway and as I put him down on the tar, all I could hear was my mother. "Leeee!"

Tears started to spill over my eyelids. With blurry vision I hit the cat with the broom sending it flying into the street. Still, it ran back to me. I shouted at it and hit it into the street again, this time harder. When it landed, it staggered towards me then paused. I was glaring at it, pointing in the other direction. "You have to go – you can't stay here anymore – now leave." I shouted.

Animals feel – I'd say even with equal depth, if not deeper than us. You know with your eyes you can lift someone's spirits or you can make them feel like a worm, you can kill a person with just a look. I wiped my eyes and Charlie and I stared at each other – there was such pain shouting out at me in his eyes – I stopped looking at him. "Leeee!" "I am coming mommy!" I said. I didn't eat breakfast, I played with my food. I started to pee in my bed quite often after this incident. I got beat for this because I'd stopped doing it a year earlier. My mother thought I was just being "lazy."

The shop wasn't leased in my aunt's name but the utilities were. Once a month my mother would leave for Kingston (Jamaica). I'd be left with the sick-minded babysitter, but anyhow, while on one such trip my aunt had the power service terminated. My mother returned to find that vultures were circling the shop; the meat in the three deep freezers had rotted. This is how spite is – it waits for god knows how long to claim its vengeance. Needless to say, my mother went to my aunt's house. She has a temper and when pissed off she doesn't think straight. During their argument my aunt revealed to my mother how "You have Charles, abusing your son" – he showed me the bruises and the tearing off of his flesh! My mother gave me a look, a look one gives to traitors. The argument abruptly ended. I was grabbed by the collar and literally dragged all the way home. Then I got an ass-whooping like I had never gotten before. I couldn't sit for days and my ribs were badly bruised. She had been punished for my treachery.

I would sneak visits to my aunt's home to get fresh produce. I'd have to pass by her house to get water from a huge storage tank that serviced the entire community. My aunt enjoyed tickling me but this one time her attempt was met by a flinch. She asked me what was wrong and I confided in her.

A month or two prior to the aforementioned final "blow up" between my aunt and my mother, my father had come to visit. He brought with him several boxes and barrels full of stuff to leave with us. I remember vividly the pleas, him begging for my mother to come back, promising his fidelity – all to no avail. Of course, my mother accepted the money he gave and all he brought with him, just not his apologies. She did however promise that she would allow him to see me when he wanted to visit and allow me to spend time with him at his residence once he got back on his feet. I remember well the last question he asked before leaving, which was basically how come she had been accepting the money he had been sending yet failed to inform him that they had broken up.

I remember the last question he asked her; "How come you have been accepting the money I have been sending for the last eight months, yet failed to inform me that we were no longer together?" My mother then pointed at me and made a sign rubbing her thumb and fingers in opposing directions, signifying "money." "It costs money to raise your son." She replied. I cried a river as I watched my father leave. Like my father, I found myself nagging and pleading for days, but only it was for his return. Another harsh ass-whooping was needed to shut me up.

Soon thereafter, my mother stripped the shop and bar of everything inside. We packed all of our belongings and moved to Kingston.

Chapter 2: The Flight to Kingston

To my distaste, my mother and Charles became more committed to one another. Charles returned to Kingston with us. We moved close to Waterhouse, it was the only area that had housing within our price range. The new place was not big enough to hold the three of us, so Charles moved with his brother uptown while we stayed in a one bedroom apartment in a tenement yard. As a rule of thumb, you didn't venture out beyond 5:00pm unless you wore a gun, which either meant you were looking to rob, steal, shoot the police, or defend drug turf. Simply put, you didn't go out.

There were raids quite often. The police's attempts to stop the flow of drugs through the docks and remove guns, and the criminals who carried them, off the streets were weak at best. During one of the raids, while gunmen scrambled through the tenement yards, a stray bullet killed a pregnant woman. The incident didn't settle well with the area don and they sought revenge on police during a road block. In response, the rat patrol, which is similar to a SWAT team, came to find the rats responsible and seek some reprisal of their own. Unfortunately for me I was walking to school that morning through the very area the confrontation was to go down. It was eerily quiet as I proceeded to the bus stop. Out of nowhere several Nissan jeeps appeared onto the scene. As the vehicles slide to a stop the officers sprung out and hit the pavement running. I found myself trapped between the men on the corner and a pack of 15 to 20 homeless and seemingly helpless young fellows. As shots rang out I did the customary thing and hit the goddamn ground! Once the shooting abated I panicked and ran towards home.

On my heels were the police as they pursued the very targets that had just targeted them.

You see, the gunmen didn't run because they were afraid, but rather to trap the police. Their plan was to draw police to an ancient drainage system that surrounds the entire area in order to counter-attack the rat patrol. As I ran there was a young man hiding behind a wall unbeknownst to the police. The officers were still on my heels and shouted my way as I ran. The young man behind the wall communicated to his fellow street crew with bird like sounds. The police were so focused on saving me from death that they did not see their own impending death coming. As the police drew nearer a young man behind a wall pointed and aimed with his right hand through a hole (in the wall). With his left arm he directed me to hit the ground. I dropped and started hollering, "Don't kill me, please don't kill me!" A loud bang followed and when I turned around I saw the young officer's head, who was once just steps behind me, blown clean off. I then stood up and the young man from behind the wall, who had just shot and killed the police, or "Babylon" as they were referred to back home, was still standing behind the wall. Once the coast was clear he grabbed me and gently placed me behind the wall and told me he would return and let me know when I could come out. He returned just a few minutes later, but it could have been an hour for all I knew. My attention was completely occupied by the dead policeman. I was about 5 years old at the time and this was only the beginning of the death and carnage I would experience over the next few years. Most would be strangers, like the lifeless policeman that lie motionless in front of me, while others would be family.

I will never forget the young man's face when he returned. He flashed me a smile and led me from behind the bricks that concealed me. He then tells me to go home as his smile quickly vanishes. He shook the revolver and patted it on his leg, looking at the dead policeman then back at me – his message was clear; "hear no evil, see no evil, and speak no evil." Another of the many rules was that if you "ratted" they would kill not only your immediately family, but also your extended family, cat, dog, babies, everything! Yes, not even your animals would be safe. With that said, or understood, I ran home and cried to my mom and told her what happened. I stammered through my words and could not speak. When I was finally able to get my words out I yelled out; "They shot the policeman!" My mother also begins to cry and tells me that she was glad that I was alright. Given what had happened, I missed school for a day and remained home. We thought it best to allow the streets to simmer down for a while.

Well, I learned to adapt real quickly, occasionally against mom's warnings. I would chat with the dudes on the corner; they called me "cheese trix" because of my complexion. To them, it resembled that of a snack that was "yellow" like Cheetos. When I ventured to the shop, I was under strict orders not to say anything or talk to no one. As soon as I turned the corner I was engaged in some conversation or another. One day while talking for a few minutes, one of the men put a hand over my mouth and said, "wa dat!" Then I heard the whistles. He said, "Shit! Babylon." That sent me packing and cleared the streets. I ran home. The JDF (Jamaican Defense Forces) only raided for a few minutes. When I made it back to the apartment I told mom that the men on the corner told me to "return home." You see, I had to speak proper as mom would not allow me to speak "patios" or Jamaican dialect in her presence. I received a slap in the mouth for saying, "dem 'tol me ti gallang ohm!" (In English: *They told me to go home*"). She said, "Me see you, how much time me 'ago tell your disobedient ass how ti no talk to 'dem, but you love bad company." She grabbed my ear, I started hollering murder as usual, and my neighbor who lived in the room up front said, "Una, wah he dun now?" (What has he done now?) She gave him that look that said, "Shut up!" He looked past the gate and saw police, then slammed his door. Well, you guessed right, while footsteps scampered outside and the shots echoed, and I got another ass-whooping which wasn't pretty.

The next body I saw was not far away, time wise. This time I was returning from school, same old routine, only this time the police shot the gunman. It's funny the police engaged their targets in the midst of civilians, which didn't help their popularity. Add to this the fact that they stopped people's "bread" and every so often shot an innocent bystander. The popular sentiment in the ghetto was not in their favor.

All of this took place in the span of three months; it was Christmas and to my surprise, guess who came around with a "trailer load?" My father! No girls this time, just toys he had bought. He had a truck full of toys for the area kids. He was usually around there every Sunday in another tenement yard a few homes down the street.

As was agreed to, I spent the holidays with him. I told him about what had happened and he followed me home to find out where I lived. He came into the yard with the bag of groceries and he and Charles met for the first time. He looked at me and he said, "Is dat 'im?" I nodded and he dropped the bags and ventured to beat the bricks out of Charles when my mother came out with a small cutlass (knife) and told him to leave. "Get out!" she shouted. "What is he doing here?" she shouted at me. Dad ventured, "Jesus Una, you left me ti dis, dis boy nearly got shot a couple of times, come back with me to Dwayne Park." My father pointed at Charles and said, "You need to stop minding him." He was ushered out and sent packing while being insulted by my mother. My mother grabbed my ear while calling me a "Goddamn chatter box!" That was my father's second to last visit.

Meanwhile mom decided she will not work for anyone, so she bought clothes, second hand shirts, corduroy pants and uniforms for hoteliers and spent hours around the sewing machine. At least in Waterhouse I returned home in time, because after dark you traveled at your own risk. Mom went to Ocho Rios and Montego Bay and sold her shirts and other clothing items. In time, she developed a clientele among Charles' co-workers. She also got the idea to start a little mobile restaurant cooking food in a construction site and selling drinks. Charles got permission from his boss to build the mobile restaurant. His boss was a big and tall funny man named "Wiggy" who would eat like you would not believe. He spoke to my mom and she convinced him that the men would not be able to leave their site and return to work on time. Then Wiggy wouldn't need the police on the site every fortnight because all of the men would be there, and nobody would come there trying to rob them with two-hundred plus men working. Most of these men came from

Waterhouse and other warrant farms. They would not allow anybody to take their money!

Eight months after returning to Kingston we moved to greater Portmore and housing scheme to a better community. I say "we" because Charles came with us. My mother became busy attending school and running the restaurant. She was home by 4:00pm. As soon as she entered the house I would be served dinner and then I would have to explain what I learned at school for the day. Most times I would leave school and go to the construction site and sit in the restaurant and do my homework.

Mom had a weird way of parenting; even though I got good grades I wasn't encouraged or congratulated. Anything less than 100% yielded punishment. An example, let's say one day I had the following subjects: Social Studies 11/14, English 12/15, Math 18/20, Integrated Science 22/25, Spelling 18/20 – for each incorrect answer I received 3 blows from the belt. If the total sum was ten incorrect, I received 30 blows with a leather strap on my hands. If I resisted, which I did most times, it was administered over my "behind."

Well, as I spent time in the restaurant, I usually walked around after I had completed my homework. Mom tried to stop me because this was a construction site and not really safe, but after repeated lectures I still disobeyed. Mom, at times, was too busy to realize I was gone anyway. I completed my homework in some corner or another, in time; I developed a friendship with a laborer called Leroy. As I got to know him, he could read my emotional responses. I remember one day after finishing my homework and calculating my incorrect answers, I sat there looking bewildered.

When I got home, I would feel the pain and hear about it. It didn't matter if I only had three, the multiplier was nine, and the blows were administered with the threat, "If you don't stop talking and wasting my money on lessons (tutoring), I am going to come to school one day and whoop your ass in front of the entire class."

I told Leroy about my dilemma and he told me to go get a red ink pen. I asked, "Why?" He just said, "Just go and get it." When I returned, he was examining my teacher's handwriting, then forged her signature and told me to do the corrections, then rewrote my grades, "Ahh." That ended mom's tirade for the next few weeks. In return, Leroy told me to get him something to eat, so I got him a bun and cheese sandwich. It was easy, I said, "Hey mom!" "Lee, I am busy!" "I'm hungry," I would say. "Okay, what do you want?" "Bun and cheese," I replied. Mrs. Green (the lady that worked with my mother) was asked to make three sandwiches. And that was that.

Leroy taught me many tricks on how to outsmart my mother. At first he asked for insignificant favors and then his requests became more bold and demanding. One day, he told me to get $50.00 as he did not have bus fare. So I stole the fifty and gave it to him. The number of "fifties" soon began to multiply and eventually he was asking every day. The little mobile eatery was a small one, and mom was a stickler for good housekeeping. Hence, she knew how every penny was spent and exactly how much she made each day. She did this by keeping a table where she had the list of meals being prepared for the week, every meal sold there would be a mark in the respective column and at the week's end, she made a tally for drinks, sandwiches, cooked foods, candy and even the clothes she sold. This was a very effective system for a small business. She soon realized that fifty dollars was missing. Then she realized one-hundred dollars was missing until eventually she realized that two-hundred and fifty dollars was missing. She then asked Mrs. Green who denied any theft, and next of course she asked me – and of course I denied it.

The trap was set for the thief and the ink was found on my hands. Mom was not only embarrassed but enraged for weeks. I got punished every day; if I slipped she got the belt. I had welts all over my body for weeks, in fact, for years. Every time I stepped out of line again I was beaten. I was told she didn't want me in her presence, so I felt betrayed. I was instructed to leave school and go straight home. As I stated before, Charles and I weren't the best of friends, so when he got a chance to punish me he did just that. He pinched, removing skin as usual, laughing as he went along. I complained to mom and that only aggravated her more. My daily dose of ass-whippings increased, literally, I got whooped every day. She was really hurt by my stealing and didn't investigate further to figure out why. Beating me was the "cure-all" for her.

If I awakened late in the morning, the belt woke me up. If I forgot to fold my clothes and place them in the proper drawer, the belt, wet rag, or extension cord met me in the shower. Whether the act was intentional or just an arbitrary mistake, she decided she was going to beat the "worthlessness" out of me. "Just like your father, you are a liar, a thief, you can't do anything right!" I endured this barrage of treatment all day, every day.

I didn't return home on time, and if I did, I sat on the veranda for hours contemplating, "Did I do anything wrong today?" I did my best at school, I started to get straight A's, but I still talked often.

This was because I was an only child; I was not allowed to play with the neighborhood kids and was forced to read, take extra classes or study some Sabbath literature being a Seventh Day Adventist.

She lived up to her word when she found out I was reprimanded at school for being an accomplice in busting a student's head. The matter is not as drastic as it sounds. We used to play "stone wars." Simply stated, we made cardboard box shields and we had three or more plastic bottles on our belts filled with stones. The objective was to take the knoll on one end of the football field, and each day the roles changed. There were attackers and defenders, and usually the defenders won, as they had a gravel pit with lots of stones that had collected from the neighbors nearby. They had dogs but that's what the stones were for, and we were able to get around the dogs. It's funny because those dogs never forgot and when given the chance, while one of us was strolling alone, the three mutts would bum-rush their victim. Many scary moments and torn pant legs can be attributed to those dogs.

On this particular occasion, a strong stone from one of the defenders hit a bystander who was at the stalls outside the school gate buying lunch. All of the boys in the class, or accomplices, then fled. My teacher, knowing the usual suspects, picked out myself, Tommy, Kevan and George. We went to the office and were beaten by the principal. We had a choice of either being suspended or being whooped. We all opted for the ass-whooping knowing that our principal could whoop us any day with much less force than at the hands of our parents, especially my mother.

We said our apologies to the young man in front of the whole school at morning devotion, and that was that. Well the tale had just begun. Kevan, my best friend at the time, was given his dose of the belt at school in front of the class by his mother. I knew once my mom did her weekly visit with my teachers, that my embarrassing moment would soon follow. When she did come to school I was doing the usual, which consisted of either playing or talking. She went to the principal's office and got my report. She had taken out her belt on the steps, shook it where I could clearly see it and then spoke to my teacher. She then took me outside for a few minutes as I explained my side of the story. This warranted a slap across the mouth and face. "When are you going to stop lying?" was her response. Of course, everyone saw what had happened and that kept me quiet for a few days. When you were teased it wasn't by only your class it was by all the kids in grades higher and lower than yours.

Now a tailor, my mom spent endless hours at the sewing machine. With her demanding work schedule requiring the bulk of her time, Charles was able to have his way with the women. The poor fool was stupid enough to get caught and the slow erosion of their relationship began. I knew he was sneaky – *just* knew it. By then my dislike had grown to full-blown hatred. I wasn't being much help. Understanding that mom was more irritable these days was not a comforting thought.

When I reviewed the days' work at school and then calculated the multiple blows that she would be serving up with added ferocity, I knew I was going to get it. She beat me just a little bit harder and with a little more heartlessness each time, as if that would make her problems somehow disappear. She blamed my misbehavior as part of the cause as to why Charles had strayed from her. So I stayed out later than usual arriving home around 8:00pm.

Charles acted mostly with indifference with one exception, when it concerned his money. You had his undivided attention; he was engaged to mom before he got caught in the act. He and my mother had pooled their resources to buy two houses on the other side of the Greater Port, but he decided he wanted to forego such arrangement, split the money, thus allowing him to take his share.

When mom was out on Saturdays, still trying to sew and run the restaurant and Charles was home, or left for the "site" after her, I would be punished for some arbitrary reason. He would pinch, I would beg him to stop, and he would laugh with a God-damned glitter to his eyes as if this was the most fun activity in the world. As usual, the pinching test (as I have come to label them) ended with a slap across the face and a shove accompanied by a closing comment, "Shut up!"

I decided that Saturday I had enough of Charles, forget mom, she was not listening to me anyway. So I was stuck somewhere between trying to please Charles and trying to keep him from hurting her. I got a long screwdriver and a knife sharpener and made myself (after a few hours of work) a long ice pick. The next time Charles decided to have a little fun with me, he was going to get a little surprise – *enough!*

Mom got Charles a job, got him his pay raised, a vehicle and pushed him to succeed. Mom refused to give him his money and so the fighting began verbally and soon escalated to real physical rumblings. As expected, I took my mother's side whenever a fight did ensue. When the fist fights began my mother's short arm reach was no match for the long reach of the 6'1" inch tall Charles.

I ran into my room and reached under my bed where I had kept the "ice pick" for safe keeping. I turned around and stormed at Charles who was standing in the hallway. Mom's back was turned toward my door as I tried to slide past her to get at Charles. She saw what was in my hand and grabbed me; in the process leaving her open to a punch. You would think that because he was older and stronger he could have stopped a 35 pound kid with a screwdriver that looked more like a sword. Charles grabbed me and started to laugh which earned him a bite on his hands. It was a bite of desperation for the fool held me in such a position that he was strangling me. He yelled, hollered, and shook his bloody hand in rage. It was too late, I hit him with my ice pick which enabled me to get on top of him and mom had a knife, and you don't want to face an angry Jamaican woman with a knife unless you are looking to be gutted like a fish.

I started shouting at him "That was for all the times you pinched me, and got away with it, you are not getting any money either, mom took you to Kingston, bought you clothes, gave you money and food, bought your tools...you piece of shit!" He stood there, so did mom. They were both focused on me and my little tirade. My mother looked astounded by what I had said, Charles looking at me as he always had done. Then he pointed with his good hand, "That little boy is going to be the death of you." Rather prophetic.

Well everything took a sudden downward turn from there on out and Charles decided mom couldn't get her furniture. She called her niece, Precious, who loved a good fight. Precious was known to fight, in fact, loved to fight and was known to throw down with the biggest of men – and had a terrible shouting game to go along with it. The only difference between Precious and most other women was that she was going to do everything she promised.

Charles had a few choices to make. He could give mom all her stuff, go to the hospital or end up in prison. He chose the most amenable solution which was to give the furniture back. Mom lied, agreeing that she would give back all his money. I think the last time I saw Charles a few years later; he was in the same house, with no electricity, no running water and still waiting for a check that would never arrive.

Precious lived in Waterhouse, basically we had run to the area we had just run from a few years earlier to move to Greater Portmore in the first place. Things had not gotten much better, easier or less violent from the look of things.

We stayed with Precious, her husband and her four children for a few months. Well, she had her own problems, mainly concerning the son in the area. She had said openly that "he was going to die there," and he was ambushed shortly thereafter. In addition to this, Precious was a staunch supporter of the PNP (People's National Party) in a JLP (Jamaican Labor Party) area.

Precious was given an ultimatum, one week to relocate or face the consequences. When you are lucky enough to be given the chance to move, you move! So she packed her stuff up, unwillingly. However, this was a young woman who had come from a hard life, worked hard to provide a decent size home for her family. She was not going to leave without a fight.

We were there the last day helping her pack all their stuff into a truck. I was posted with Precious' older daughter who gave the warning, "dem coming." Instead of hurrying or speeding up the pace, Precious stormed for the gate, knife in hand. Mom grabbed me and we jumped the fence. In a few minutes, the argument and fight ended in 9 bangs as I watched through a hole in the fence, 9 shots to Precious' head, or what was left of it after the first slug had hit her.

Her husband fled with his child, the youngest of the siblings, while the other three suffered. Mom and I fled to Mrs. Green's for shelter. Seems we picked the wrong places for lodging. The landlord and Mrs. Green were already on bad terms and he demanded, "If more people are going to occupy this place I want more money."

It wasn't long before the inevitable happened, Mrs. Green and her landlord locked horns and Mom joined on Mrs. Green's side. The landlord got cut in the process and ran saying he was going to return, and next time he was going to "kill something!"

Mrs. Green fled to friends, Mom with her, but we forgot to take some clothes. So Mom decided she had to sneak into the home to get the clothes, her money and her handbag. The landlord was posted there as soon as we entered. We did not enter through the front gate but over the backyard fence and walked around the corner of the house. Ours eyes locked on a man with a bandage on his arm and something that looked like black metal in his hand. He pointed and shouted and we took off. In the process my mom and I were separated.

I walked aimlessly looking for my mother, the police were about to do a raid and I went into the midst of them, grabbing an officer's shirt. I told him that my mom and I got separated and explained the entire exodus since Greater Portmore.

The officers returned to Mrs. Green's rent-a-shack and after asking a few questions of the neighbors, soon reunited me with my mom. They then gave my mother some words of advice, "You need to get this child out of this area, because this is no place to raise him."

We only had one place left to go and that was to leave the country, leave Kinston altogether. Mom went to find Precious' second child and her favorite "protected child in the world", and off to St. Elizabeth (another parish in South Western, Jamaica) we went. We found lodging at my grandmother's, who was taking care of another older woman. She told us we could stay as long as we wished. It was here that mom hatched the idea of immigrating to the United States and she decided to ask her cousins for help. The only question was whether or not my cousin would even talk to my mom. They had been feuding for nearly five decades.

We went to my Grand Aunt Ilene's place and talked, mom got reacquainted with her estranged family members and I was introduced to some second cousins. On our next visit my mom decided to ask Peggy for help, who was the oldest of Aunt Ilene's children. But before ever asking she all of a sudden changed her mind and was preparing to leave instead. When I realized this I ran to Cousin Peggy, grabbed her blouse and started pulling her to the veranda. Mom had turned back to get me. They met in the driveway and I looked at mom with a smirk, "Go ahead and ask her!" "Ask me what?" said Peggy. The discussion progressed from there. Peggy decided she would willfully help my mother, by giving her a place to stay and show her the ropes in St. Maarten (a Dutch/French island in the Eastern Caribbean). Mom found a friend who would keep me, Veronica, an old classmate at the school she attended to become a seamstress.

I looked at mom at the airport and she started to cry; she bent downward, I wiped her eyes, "See mom, I am not crying because you are leaving to create a better life for us." I wiped away some more of her tears, hugged her, she laughed, looked at me and walked away. It was a good thing she didn't turn around because I had begun to cry myself. Silently beads of tears rolled down my face. I didn't let out any sounds but I did continue crying, watching my mom grow smaller and smaller in the distance. A true statement, because that gap over the years would only grow greater, that void in me would never be filled.

Chapter 3: Rolling Stone

The first place I went was Barbican, Kingston. I tried my best to settle into my new home. The house was small and surrounded by a zinc fence with a quarter-acre backyard. In the back is where Barry, Veronica's common law spouse, planted vegetables for the market. Veronica placed me in a new school, Barbican Primary School, and I held my own but was still quite the "chatterbox."

Barry didn't work and so could not contribute much to the household income. Veronica was a self-employed tailor who ran a shop with her sister as her business partner. I spent most of my weekends at the shop.

After a month or so, Veronica and Barry had their first real fight. Veronica had just given birth to Barry's child just eight months earlier, but he would not try to find work because he preferred to stay home and take care of the baby, cook and clean. Since he *was not* the bread winner he *could not* order Veronica around.

Every month my mother would send money, U.S. dollars, and Veronica had full control over how the money was spent. She decided to save it and just had me eat whatever they were having. Barry had other thoughts on how the money should be used.

Each day I had chores which I willingly performed most of the time. Well, until this one day where I came home to a sink full of dishes. Barry pointed to them and I replied, "Who me?" He says, "Yeah! Wash them!" I explained to him, "Look man, you're home all day, clean, cook and watch soap operas, how hard can that be?

School is hard work too; you've been home all day!" He says, "Shut up and start the dishes!" I then turn to walk away in order to sit my backpack down and he grabs me by my collar and slaps me across the head. I jerk away and told him, "You are worthless; you only beat up little children. You call yourself a man?"

He knew what I meant. In the last fight I saw, Veronica was doing the laundry and as soon as he opened his mouth, she took his drawers in her hand and smacked him across the face. That statement earned me a slap in the face and a few punches on my arms. The blows made my left arm go limp as he continued to hit me with a strap for "giving him the lip."

When Veronica came home she shouts for me in usual fashion bearing a variety of snacks and pastries. Only this time I didn't come running, but instead she finds me crumpled in a corner of the bedroom. She saw the scratches on my face and welts on my arms as well as the fist marks on my shoulders and hands. She immediately goes looking for Barry. She finds him on the sofa and grabs him and pulls him off; "What the fuck did he do to earn that beating?" He shoved her off saying, "The boy has no manners, I told him to do something and he back answered. I put him in his place; bet him he won't be doing it again." Well the argument did not stop there. And to make clear the situation and physical features of our combatants, Veronica is what we call a "mampi" (a very large Jamaican woman). She stood around 6'1" tall and weighed about 300 pounds. However, she was quick, really quick with fists like cinderblocks and she knew exactly how to use them. Barry was a scrawny, 6'2", slimly built, with a receding hair line. He was basically in shape enough to get knocked out. A fight ensues but not for long, as Barry was quickly overwhelmed by the hurricane of cinderblocks. Afterwards, I am given a lecture not to say anything out of the way to Barry. Of course after his own beating he was itching for me to do anything wrong. He would whip me for all sorts of stuff; not shining the floors correctly, doing the laundry wrong, not cleaning my school shoes – mostly arbitrary offenses and minor slip ups. It was like a domino effect, every time I got punished by Barry, he was punished by the mampi the very same day. If Veronica happened to be home, the fight would begin immediately. Stated simply, Barry didn't like me. Every day I would have belt buckle marks on my body, along with bleeding welts and palm sized black and blue bruises.

I started coming home later when I knew Veronica was there. That way Barry would not touch me. He took on the burden of finding me - the ever caring parent; bringing me home by the ear, then giving me some chore or another. I had to weed his garden, do the laundry, do the dishes, clean the house, but of course he would find a mistake. He'd utter, "You know, don't cha now, eh!" Sometimes I would escape red all over, giving him a piece of my tongue when I was far enough away. It got to the point where Veronica, for the sake of keeping the peace, would tell him that she would punish me so he didn't have to. But of course he didn't fall for it. Whenever his beatings get out of hand, meaning above black and blue spots all over, she would beat him up. She finally said, "It is settled, I am beating him with the strap." I just had to live with a few welts and buckle marks.

One weekend Barry sells all his produce at the market and forces me, a small 40 lb. kid, to push a 35 lb. wheelbarrow filled with callaloo (a relative of spinach). In his hand was a small switch that he carried to use in the same manner as a jockey's whip if and when I slacked off.

Unable to take anymore, I wrote to my mother and begged for her to get me away from there. Finally in the summer she sent me to my father's place. Now, they were not at all on good terms, but Veronica had told her that she had to move me because the arrangement was just not working out.

While at my dad's place, mom calls and tells me that I am coming to St. Maarten for the holidays. She asked dad if he would keep me when I return but he said, "No." My time in St. Maarten was spent basically having fun, since mom worked cleaning houses 3 days a week and also worked at a shoe store. I had somewhat of a new step-father who took a liking to me. All was going well until we got hit by a large Hurricane. The storm took both our home and what little furniture my Mom had. She had exhausted all efforts to keep me in St. Maarten with limited recourse being that we were there illegally. Therefore it was difficult for her to find a school for me to attend. Having no other choice she writes my Aunt Marie and asks if she would keep me. My Aunt agrees to step in and help, and just like that I was in a cab and on my way to Endeavor. When I arrived to my Aunt's place she greeted me at the front gate, along with her two daughters, Carlena and Stacy, who were both older high school students. I brought along with me a few suitcases and several hundred (United States) dollars. For the first month or so everything went smoothly. There were 20 acres of farmland which included goats, pigs, planted yams, and sweet potatoes. There was an orchard with tangerines, grapefruits and oranges. The hillsides were filled with blackberry bushes that grew year-round. I had enrolled in school at Gibraltar and was placed in grade six.

Aunt Marie complained that my mom had not sent any money after my two months of living with her. Soon after I would come to learn that my Aunt was ten times more abusive than my mother – not to mention neglectful and downright mean at times. Eventually she grew tired of my "lip" as she would say. I was just the kind of fellow who asked a lot of questions. When I got a whooping, she really "tore my ass up." She was a very irrational and eccentric woman, gentle only when she wanted to be and when she was in a good mood. Although the punishments I received from her were worse than my mother's, they were both the same when it came to being moody. My Aunt Marie's mood swings, though, were much more volatile and intimidating.

While her daughters went to school, I spent nearly half of one semester on the farm. I had a pair of khaki pants and one khaki shirt. They were both worn and torn after a while with patches all over. A neighbor, Ms. Donna (the same lady discussed earlier on whose son, Kamas, I would take to school) had saved for me another set of uniforms. Her house was the only other place I was allowed to visit and I practically lived there. Many days when my aunt's house was empty with nothing but bloody potatoes, Ms. Donna would leave my dinner and I would change clothes from school there. My routine was pretty much the same every day, which consisted of doing my homework, eating dinner, and watching television. I would talk to anyone whose first words when I opened my mouth were not, "Shut up!"

Ms. Donna really looked out for me. All the clothes that I had originally brought with me I eventually gave away. And it wasn't that I was being foolish in giving my clothes away – I mean, what could I do with twelve dozen t-shirts that were about five years old? Mom called them "grow into clothes" – "Yeah, right." What I didn't give away was in a pile somewhere around the yard, my laundry was rather neglected.

As for my cousins…hmm, very interesting. Let's see, I was nine years old when I was truly introduced to sex. Carlena was the very first time. It was a Saturday evening and my Aunt Marie was gone, and the house was empty except for us two. I was lying on the bed next her and doing my homework when out of nowhere she kisses me. I had no idea how to kiss not to mention I didn't want to in the first place. I recoiled and jumped off of the bed. I found the whole tongue in the throat and choking thing repulsive. By the time I caught my breath she was kissing me again. The next time it happened I was in the bathroom taking a bath, yet another Saturday, when the door opened. The lock was broken on the door so anyone could just wander in. I had just boiled a large pan of water and filled the tub with two buckets from the tank (water caught from rain). I was milking a bar of soap trying to make a bubble bath when I heard the door; "Creeeeek!!" "What are you doing?" I said. By the end of the sentence she (Carlena) was in the tub, this and other advances went on until I finally went along with the program.

Now let's see, my other cousin Stacy was way more aggressive than her sister. She would simply make her demand "Lee, come here!" I would go and the door closed. Click! Click! Bam! She would be on the bed with the key to unlock the door in her hands and tell me to "Come and get it!" "Look Stacy, I am going to tell Aunt Marie." "Yeah, like she will believe you." You see, Stacy was high-yellow, Indian and Aunt Marie's favorite. The child could do no wrong in her eyes.

Stacy had a very bad temper, plus she outweighed me since she was 8 years older. Myself, scrawny, and as I said, the cabinet was empty and I hadn't yet sharpened my fighting skills. So I would try to wrestle for the key – getting punched, shoved, slapped – all lightly at first, then she would slap me, throw me on the bed, tear off all my clothes and hold me under the blankets. She held the key in her left hand and gave me two orders, "Eat me or fuck me!" I'd look at her, disinterested and she'd say, "You want the key or not, you are not leaving until you do it, you might as well." Then she would spread her legs open, hold my head and I would punch her, a bad mistake. I always punched anyway, she would smirk as if to say "Yeah, that's the way you like it." She would overpower me and I would just take it.

As I said, Stacy was a bully; Aunt Marie would leave chores to share but Stacy had other plans. Any work she would dump off on Carlena or on me. Carlena and I would grab broomsticks and have an all-out brawl with Stacey when it came to matters such as these. One very memorable day, the three of us were slugging it out. I stepped back and looked at the avocadoes on the counter in plain view. Carlena was getting in some good blows while the whole time Stacy laughed and smirked. In an instant I grabbed the pile of avocados and "bulla" (pastry) and took off! I ran out to the tangerine orchard which was covered with heavy vines. I had made my own little entrance and exit to escape Stacy. She figured out I was at the orchard, got the cutlass and began yelling, "You piece of shit…" cutting her way around the orchard, swinging for my head. I knew my way around the inside of my little "nest haven" really well. Inside the nest were pots, pans, salt, pepper and other seasonings. I made crushed seasoning from bird pepper (wild) and kept a few utensils. When I did shoot a dove or parrot (parakeet) to eat, I'd steal some green banana or plantains and cook me up a little pepper pot. With the help Ms. Donna, along with stealing and berry hopping, I was able to consume enough to at least come out looking human. Nonetheless, I was still very skinny because you could only steal so many times from the same place before being caught. I would do my thieving at night. I stopped moving the pigs around regardless of how much Aunt Marie beat me. We had a boar, yes the darn thing had tusks and one day I was moving it and eating some blackberries – unbeknownst the darn pig attacks me. *So who says Nile crocs are the only animals that actively hunts people?* This pig bites me! I hollered until I got some help and when it was all said and done I walked away with just a few cuts and bruises. Boy did I do that hog some good, I'd beat that pig every chance I got. I cut a club out of the hills in the backyard made especially for him.

At school I did rather well. Some hated me, some loved me or at least we got along. I was an amicable fellow, quick to make others laugh, help others out, but still not the class clown. When it came time for common entrance exam, I took extra classes for two months and with the help of Ms. Donna's tutoring, I passed with flying colors.

I did have my problems with peers, namely this fellow named Gregory. We could not stand each other for some reason.

The dame of the class was a beautiful young lady we called "Miss Mack." I never got around to letting her know that I liked her because I was too shy. The other guy, Gregory, liked her as well. In fact, all the boys seemed to be drawn to her beauty.

So one day Greg bounces into her and she pushed him off and tells him, "Leave me alone, I don't like you." Greg didn't take to this too kindly and therefore picked a fight. I couldn't mind my own business nor was I trying to show off as he was larger and much more muscular than I was at the time. However, he was not too bright. I stepped between them and told Greg to stop, he shoved me out of the way and went on. Ok! I tapped him on the shoulder saying, "Hey punk!" Well the challenge for the lady, or so I thought, was on. I was in the gaze of Miss Mack giggling at my side, laughing. If my recollection is correct, she was laughing at Greg. I was told the culprit knocked me out with a solid mahogany handle cricket bat. I said I was told this by my best friend Kenroy, because I do not remember a thing. My head was swollen and I was in and out of consciousness with headaches for a few days. I didn't go to the doctor, though. I got bitters, bush medicine, and some sleep. In three days I was as good as new, minus the giant head scab. Once all healed up I returned to school and quietly ignored Greg. I cornered him at lunch time when he was all by himself, he apologized and made up. "We're cool, right?" "Uh huh, sure we're cool!" I said. Then I called him out loudly, "Don't have your cricket bat now do ya pal?"

He got me a few more times, not up close, but with his sling shot. I caught up with him sooner or later with a bottle mixed with water and poison ivy. That was the end of that. He didn't bother me anymore.

Aunt Marie had decided upon mom's return that she'd never keep me again. I was too, "disobedient and stubborn." "No matter how much you beat him, he just won't listen and him still chat back!" So that was the end of my stay with her.

Mom congratulated me on passing, showed me my prize – a super Nintendo. I wouldn't get to play it because, well, I gave all my clothes away. That act warranting an airing out (yelling) from my mom. After a few minutes of brooding over this, she was in no mood for games. She was 180 lbs and hit like a Mack truck. The first blows would disable your hands from trying to defend them, no more welts, just marks on my shoulders and outer chest, that hurt a lot more, and took a long time to heal, and much more memorable. That beating straightened me out for a day or two.

Mom brought me a 25 pound turkey for my birthday and my Aunt Marie did the carving. This is the hilarious part. I am served dead last, guess what I get – two wings! Mom was looking all along and had a grand fit when Aunt Marie put the two "flippers" on my plate. Mom yelled, "Don't touch it, don't touch it Lee! Good God, no wonder the boy is so skinny, right in front of my face, his own birthday gift and you give him two wings?" "I wonder what you did to him behind my back." She went on and on until she packed us up. Well not yet, I went to Ms. Donna, she wanted to keep me, but my aunt being in such close proximity would give reason for more arguments. I cried, I loved Ms. Donna, but I said my goodbyes and we left.

Chapter 4: Next Stop Trysee

A longtime friend of my mother's lived within the vicinity of my high school. Her name was Sonia Hodges, but we just called her Pearla. Pearla had known me since I was a toddler at Oakland Road. The first few months with her went leisurely along. I was eleven years old when I entered the gates of York Castle High School, filled with dreams and aspirations long gone. Mom sewed my uniforms, khaki pants and shirts and took a lot of pictures, then departed as usual. Pearla had two children, well, two grown children. The first was daughter Tika who was in her second year of college and spent most of the year in Kingston where she went to school. The other child, Marvin, was around 22 or so at the time and attended community college.

My school was a good 2 mile trot each morning. I would awake at 5:00am and prepare myself. I would always arrive before 7:45am, but school didn't begin until 8:15am. Much of my first semester was spent frolicking around. I did poorly and placed 25th out of a total of 53 students. The next semester was not much better at a mere 20th, and then I was stuck from there between 10th and 15th in my class.

Though I spent much of my time talking, I was still not the class clown. I participated in all my classes, did my housework, I just wouldn't study. I enjoyed research and group projects. I spent lots of time at the library with my best friend Brian. I will describe him briefly since he was a fair student like me and enjoyed only a few subjects at which he excelled. The sciences were his favorite subjects; he was also a good literature student and because of his bookish nature he earned the title of "nerd." He was a very calm and dependable individual. Come to think about it, I think I might still owe him a few bucks.

I participated in volleyball, cricket, football and table tennis. I spent a lot of time drawing charts, symbols and creating artwork to beautify our classrooms. I was always assigned to clean the class at least twice a week.

I had a little trick that I had started in grade 7; each Valentine's Day I would purchase, beforehand, three bags of rose petals (yellow, white and red) and a pack of small hallmark cards and if I had enough money, some cheap chocolates. I'd sneak away from devotion (morning worship) and stick a rose, card and chocolate in some girls' bag or sweater.

I had my girlfriend, Kedian; I can freely say she knows me more intimately than anyone else. With her I discussed my dreams, fears, family problems and future concerns openly. She was quiet, never yelled, studious, adventurous in her own way and very expressive – though she kept that a secret. She was one of the only consistent figures in my life. We agreed that we'd abstain from sex, as we were both Christians and I explained that I wouldn't want any child, especially mine, to live the life that I've had to live. Being a teenage father didn't fit within my vision of a future. I also told her that my mother would kill me if I became a father prematurely.

There were three people who would see through my façade: Kedian, Brian and Nevino. From the beginning, my friends and I were bullied; we were small in stature, full in mouth, and hung out by ourselves. We got "grubbed" (teased) by the older boys, normally seniors; some were even "prefects" (students who were given positions of responsibility because of their exemplary behavior in all areas).

We were caught one day in the auditorium's restroom, our pockets ransacked and all our lunch money stolen. We complained to our homeroom teacher, Ms. Maxwell, who did her best to resolve our grievances. Unfortunately, that did not help our situation as our antagonists persisted even more so because we had "snitched."

We quit using the restroom and found some corner or another to urinate. We avoided the auditorium for a while. This persisted until I was placed in a particularly embarrassing situation. I had ventured into the restroom; my antagonists came out of their stalls, held my hands behind my back and searched my pockets. "You got no money." I told them a few obscenities which earned me a slap or two. They then removed my shoes and socks and "voila," there went my lunch money. Down to my last recourse, I spat in one of the young men's faces. The guy restraining me laughed which afforded me enough leeway. I got one hand loose and punched the guy kneeling in front of me who was wringing my ear - right in the kisser, splitting his lip.

I was rewarded for my actions with a smack across the head. When I got up, I was thrown into a stall; they each urinated in the toilet, and then they took turns dousing my head. They kept me in their toilet bowl of urine while they flushed it. "What do you think of that punk, next time just give it to me when I ask you!" I didn't go to the office, two of the accomplices were prefects, plus I had already exhausted that remedy. I told Marvin who told his older brother and they cornered the bully, smacked him around a few times and warned him, "When you see him, you leave him the fuck alone. Next time I am going to break your fucking hand, and tell all your friends we come from Trysee." I think he got the message and soon his friends were protecting me.

Trysee Village was known for violence. Most of the residents of that community were once residents of Kingston or had relatives in Kingston. The area was raided occasionally as police would come in search of one suspect or another hiding out there. The police did not venture into Trysee Village unless it was absolutely necessary.

On weekends most of my time was spent behind the counter. Pearla owned a small retail outlet. I would take my homework along; mostly I was there on Sunday afternoons. She had quite a bit in common with my mother, so much so that the same rules applied. You go to school stay in the house and you are not allowed to socialize with the neighborhood kids.

One Sunday after serving behind the counter for an hour or so, I was relieved to go home. I had been warned by both Pearla and Marvin to go straight to the house. Figuring since my homework was completed, laundry done, and my uniforms ironed, why not play some cricket or football. I was carrying the label of "nerd" and I wanted to lose the "overhead." Upon consideration the soccer field is right in front of Pearla's shop, I decided against outdoor sports. I went inside the community center and played some handball. A discussion arose about planes; the conversation was an open one so I jumped right in. Taking over the conversation, I starting with the Wright Brothers and went on to discuss the B-17, B-52, P-51 Mustangs, Germany's last attempt at the jet fighter, to the Mig-29, etc. During my "lecture" I was mainly debating against one fellow named Shawn. I was used to debating and ate him for lunch, the conversation dies and I win.

Shawn and I played another game of hand ball, but he played rather aggressively, using me as a target. I decided I had it when he intentionally aimed at my head and I got hit in the eye. I walked away, actually quitting the game, but I was losing anyway. He hung around like a wasp... nag! nag! nag! I then made my way out to the steps at the front of the community center. He follows me there along with his "tagalongs." After an hour or so of sitting alone, I decided to take sides in a 3 on 3 slap boxing.

I won and Shawn took my opponent's position. He was not only five years older than I was but also much bigger. He had stronger arms and a much longer reach. He toyed with me, a fake, a smack, the aim was to get in only face slaps. He continued to toy with me; I was smaller and faster but still couldn't get inside. He would drop his arms and stick his chin out, teasing me to hit it. I weaved to the opposite side where I was rewarded with another smack and some more taunting. I decided that I couldn't get him, so I became defensive and let him attack me.

I bobbed, weaved and ran in circles. He got frustrated and I made the circle larger and larger. The circle of his friends, who were at the edge of the ring at the beginning of the fight, began to shrink. I got cornered and punished with some combinations. After a few good hits, he stuck his cheek out and dropped his arms. This was the only time I caught him and caught him good! My fingerprints sunk deep into his face. The crowd began cheering me on as I tried to pin him down and get him to tap out. The only way to win was for the other person to call it quits. I grabbed his legs and he buckled. I tried to grapple for his hands, but he outmaneuvered me and grabbed my neck putting me in a deep hold. A trick I learned from my swimming class at the YMCA was about a particular pressure point located between the tendons of the elbow. This caused him to scream and temporarily paralyzed his arm. He was in pain for sure as he stood there and held his arm. *Rap! Rap!* I quickly delivered two licks across his face! After that he went bezerk. I tried to hold my own but I was shorter, smaller, and simply overwhelmed. He hit me a couple times in the ribs and with a few more slaps, lip-busting slaps; and that was all she wrote. Some of the older kids were outside and had joined in watching the fight. Being that I was the loser, I immediately became eligible to be "grabbed" (the tearing off of your clothes).

I was divested of all my clothes, standing there bare naked for all to see. Talk about humiliating! They gave my clothes to my peers who seized the opportunity to taunt me. They took my clothes and ran into the field. I had two choices, try to pass these grown men on the back door (that was not happening) or go get my clothes. I chose the way of more resistance since the "center" was close to my house by just a few paces. A good trot and no one would see me. So I ran outside and attempted to enter the lane that led to safety and my clothes. They both outpaced and outflanked me. I was pushed and shoved in the direction of the soccer field where my jeering peers held up my clothes like an odd trophy. I glanced at the field and there were girls around, and therefore running through the 800 meter wide landscape was an option I'd rather avoid. I decided to continue after my garments. As the teasing continued one of the older guys present stuck out his cheek and I kicked him in the chin.

The other guys taunted him and cheered me on, giving me the name, "Chung Lee."

I was quite fond of Karate movies. A fellow grabbed the top of my head, holding me at arms' length. He then reached and took hold of both of my ears and used them to lift me off the ground. The pain was tremendous and he eventually dropped me back down. They all stood around laughing. I was crumpled there, holding my ears and whimpering in pain. In a few minutes I recovered and was more determined than ever to get my clothes back. As I saw a crowd gathering around me for more laughing and taunting, I got up and flailed wildly, scratching, punching, and doing whatever and eventually I got through. To make matters worse they created an opening in the crowd and dared me to cross it. Every time I got close to passing, a slap from some older student sent me flying backwards to where I had been a few seconds earlier. I kicked one of my antagonists in his gonads and he went down! They shouted; "Damn it, Chung Lee is mad!" Another push, another slap and two blows to my thighs paralyzed my legs, now I crumpled. "Come on, don't you want your clothes back?" someone said while holding my boxer shorts in the air. Eventually I recovered and took the easiest way out, I turned toward the field. I was at the end of my patience and except for Shawn and his gang; everybody either got out of my way or joined in getting my clothes back piece by piece. Although I never recovered my entire uniform, I was able to retrieve my boxer shorts. Marvin must have heard the rumors or seen me running butt naked chasing Shawn and company to get my clothes. He came out of the shop, got my clothes and said, "You won't listen, will you?"

Mom returned that summer and I told her that I didn't want to return to Pearla's. I told her about the incident which got me another dose of the belt for disobedience. Then, as usual, she added some extras for all the other wrongs I had committed either at school, Pearla's, or somehow disrespecting her. And although my request to leave Pearla's caused me a little pain, in the end it was granted and for that it was worth it.

Chapter 5: True Love Lives Here

My mother decided to ask another estranged family member if she could keep me. She turned to her Aunt Blossom. My mother had taken care of Aunt Blossom's daughters while she was teaching, so a favor was due. Aunt Blossom had stated that she didn't know if it would be a wise decision because she had health issues that she was dealing with at the time. Additionally, her husband works most days. Her oldest daughter, Simone, volunteered to keep me. She had just graduated from a teaching college and we bonded quite easily. In a week or two, I was living at my grand aunt's residence. She had a total of three daughters who were Melene, Simone, and Ophelia. We all got along with sheer ease, I was introduced to a vegan diet, which I enjoyed and we attended church weekly. The entire family was Seventh Day Adventists.

Simone had a parenting style that was the complete opposite of any approach I had encountered before. We sat down, and she asked me what I expected from her. She saw the look of astonishment on my face when she uttered this statement, as my expression said, "What?" Then she explains that she wasn't going to do this or that. She would not beat me, we would create a contract. I keep my end of the bargain and she will keep hers. She went on to explain that she will not lie to me, spend lots of time doing activities with me and be there to listen. She smiled, laughed and explained her end of the bargain. She asked that I listen to her, and remember that as my guardian, she is responsible for me. I will not always agree with her decisions, but she would be open to listening and making any necessary changes in her life to accommodate me and find a compromise. She always wanted me to know that I could speak to her openly and freely and discuss any problems with her. All the things I had thought I would never hear.

Her actions are always pro-active. She encouraged me and when I was wrong, she explained and commented how well I had been doing. She pointed out my strong points, then showed me why so and so was wrong, then gives me as much time as needed to cross-question and actually comprehend what she was saying.

She never once raised her voice, never shouted, and I did my best to give her no reason to do so. She got a job at Spalding High School. We moved to a small studio apartment at one of her old acquaintances. By old acquaintance I mean that the landlord was a retired education administrator.

Simone taught computer science and information technology to the senior class. We travelled by bus to school. She realized from the beginning the unreasonableness of having me travel from my high school (which was 7-9 bus rides). These buses were packed like sardine cans. The sign would say, "Licensed to carry 30 passengers," but there would be 75 people smashed together on each bus. I was actually performing terribly because I would be too tired by the time I reached school, which dictated that I rise at 3:30am, leave at 4:30am at the latest, to catch the empty buses, but that never happened because everyone got up early to do this. I would reach Brownstown by 6:30am.

Simone decided it would be best to transfer me to her school, Spalding High School, since she was on the staff there. I would be much closer to home and thus would be better for both of us. We cooked together, played board games, read, studied Bible lessons and homework. She had put a few plans for further education on the back burner because she said that could take too much of her time and thus negate her responsibilities to me.

She received only the money my mother left with us, including several boxes of crackers, noodles, cheese and canned beans. At first, Simone had started out at the lowest pay rate (even below regular salary) and teachers were not compensated well to begin with – a worldwide trend I have come to observe. After two to three months, she was given the regular salary.

She decided that we would move to a new apartment in Spalding which was located within walking distance of the school. It was a two bedroom apartment, so I had my own room. This was too bad because I was in her room most of the time and slept there most nights. She would usually be on the bed marking papers, reading, studying or wrestling with me.

I fit in my new class like a perfectly matching puzzle piece. I excelled, did very well, made new friends, had a ball and life was perfect – could not be any better. Simone would stay an hour or two after school to help other students. She jumped right into a class that was designed to prepare students for graduation since they had lost a teacher for a few months and she needed the extra work.

I made myself helpful by acting like a book keeper - cleaning up, arranging things around the apartment and doing my homework. Most of my homework was already completed in class, a habit I had developed years ago. I would look in the corner of the blackboard that showed what we needed to do for the night then go to those pages, zooming through the work while my memory of the material was still fresh. Simone taught me that method. After school, I would review my work. This made studying and retaining much easier.

After my homework was finished, I would often head home and eat my dinner that had already been prepared. Most times, she was still helping her weaker students, especially those who didn't have access to a computer at home. Then I would go to the back of the apartment complex and chew on some papayas, plums or coco fruit. Then I would go about doing my chores. I would sweep, clean the toilet bowl, straighten up my room, and clean up the mess I had created in the living room. I rarely did the dishes because I hated doing dishes.

I usually spent all evening with Simone until I fell asleep. Sometimes I would awake before her and wake her by kindly nipping her nose. She would awake, blind a few minutes, only to be greeted by my weirdest, "Good Morning!"

One night, we were sitting playing games and talking when I heard a knock. She asks me to see who it was at the door. I went to the door and saw my mom standing there. I took to my heels running in the opposite direction. I ran behind Simone and shouted, "She's going to take me away!" Simone told me to calm down and that I was just being silly. My mom stood at the door and watched me and Simone conversing. I even touched Simone as if she was my mother. My mom comes home and I am not even appreciated. She talked rapidly to Simone, who was completely taken aback wondering where the sudden hostility was coming from. She tried to answer all my mother's questions to no avail. My mother stalked around the house, ripping doors open and pointing out objects and things; making a fuss about the unwashed laundry, the food in the refrigerator, accusing Simone of doing something to her son. She said, "Who gave you the authority to move Lee?" Before Simone could even explain, she was fired on with yet another set of vile remarks.

Simone finally had to raise her voice for the first time. I had never heard her raised voice. She got my mother quiet for one second, and then she pointed out, "If I knew your address, then I would have informed you. For five months you have sent no money and we have been living entirely off my salary." She went on to say,

"Lee is healthy, happy and doing well in school. Have you ever asked him what he's thinking or how he feels?"

Mom replied, "Lee, I am going and you are coming." I then replied; "No, I am staying with Simone!" I spent the night with Simone, but mom returned in the morning and started packing up my stuff. Simone said, "Are you taking him for the holiday?" She got a grunt for a reply.

Simone tried to make the situation as amicable as possible. She showed her my school reports and compared them to last semester's grades. The replies came only as grunts or stares. Mom then took a camera and took pictures of me, the house, the refrigerator and the unwashed bag of laundry. If she had asked, the laundry was not done because the water had been off for a week due to the pipes needing to be fixed. We could not carry enough water upstairs to do laundry, only enough in small containers to cook and shower.

Well, as I had predicted, it all went down and mom moved me to the country for the summer. She beat the living nonsense out of me. "How dare you choose her over me, I am your mother!" She threatened that if I ever contacted Simone again that I would "get more of where that came from" and pointed to the welts already on my arms.

I dared to ask, "What is the purpose of moving me?" A slap was her reply, "Because I am your mother and what I say you do!" Then she added, "While I was talking to Simone she told me that when you grow up that you have some things to tell me. So go ahead and tell me right now, so I can stop bothering with you, you ungrateful bastard." Then I got the, "If it weren't for you," lecture I had heard 1,000 times. These words were accompanied by the "beating the worthlessness out of you" routine. Then she beat me for being secretive and not talking with her. Every time I opened my mouth, I was rewarded with a stare, slap or some form of punishment.

I got beatings at least twice daily for a few good hours with my mouth closed, so imagine the trouble I would have caused myself had I opened it. Nope, that was not going to be worth it. The abuse was a 24 hour a day thing (verbal and physical). A lecture about my disobedience, being worthless, being heartless, causing her to become a failure, coupled with how I was to be blamed for all her failed relationships including her current relationship which was now in disarray.

She cursed because I would not eat. She cursed because I would stand at the fridge and remove out what I needed to make a sandwich and re-heat some cooked food. I would replace the object I removed to its original position, but get an ass-whopping for: using dirty hands to open the refrigerator, leaving two crumbs, or not replacing utensils or cookware perfectly - the knife, the pot – had to be in their exact proper positions. If it was two inches away from where it was supposed to be, I got it some more. It was like she walked around the place with a tape measure. It was pure hell.

As I stated, it was hell. If I moved, I got punished, so I sat in a corner and pretended to read and when she was not around, I cried. I made sure not to let her see me crying, as that would be followed by yet another all too familiar dialogue, "You want me to give you something to cry about. You have the best life, yet you are an

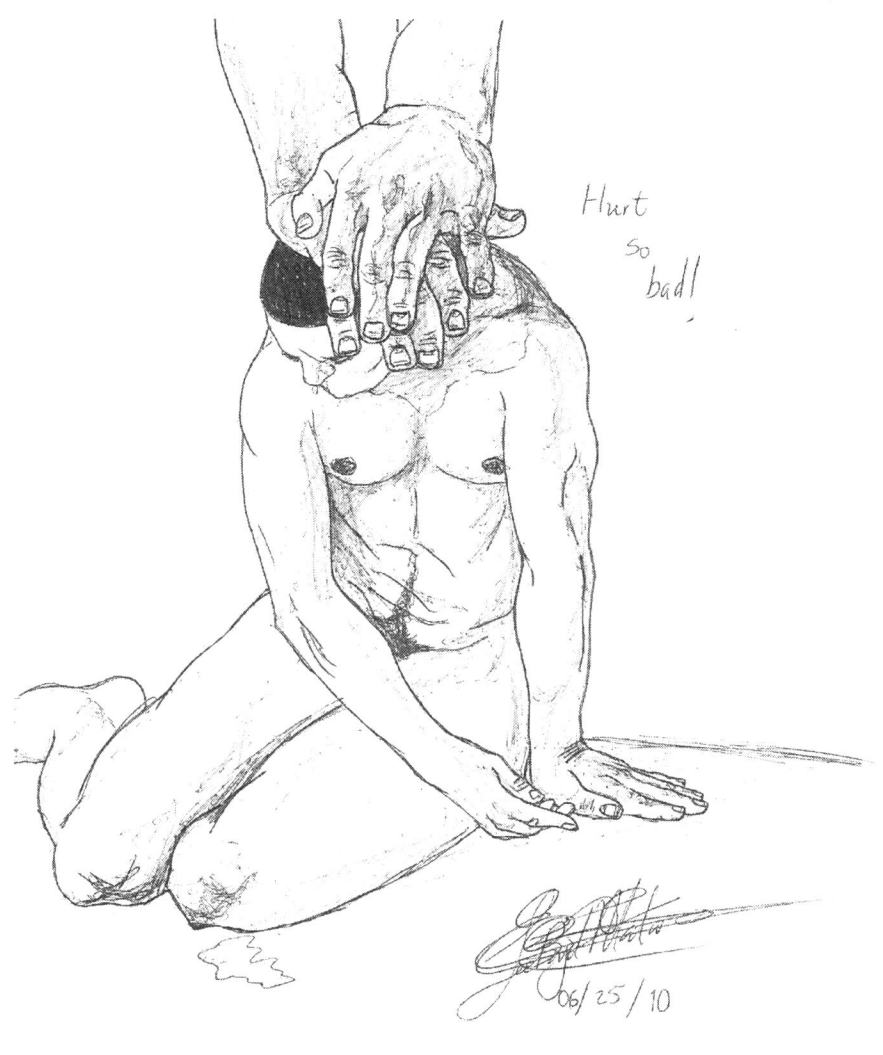

ungrateful piece of shit, just like your father, worthless!" She'd continue, "Why can't you be good and make yourself useful? Who are you looking at? You had better straighten your face before I straighten it for you." "You are nothing but a lackadaisical lazy ass, boy." On and on she would go. I could not sit in peace without being chastised and punished; the beatings would usually end with, "I am your mother!"

If we went out shopping in the supermarket and helped someone out or read the label for an old lady, she would not commend me for anything. Fortunately for me, she had to leave for a while. She found a boarding home which was a stone's throw from York Castle High School. I was transferred right back to that wretched place! She left again, this time leaving me with the Robinson's. "Just let me get a bad report from them and see what I do to you." No hugs, no kisses, just threats of violence. "Goodbye and you better write!"

Chapter 6: The Robinson's

The Robinson's board home was located about a hundred paces from the York Castle High School. I was transferred and returned to my old class. The class and school I did not like.

The Robinson's were yet another heavily Christian-based environment. The husband, Mr. Robinson, was a pastor of a small Pentecostal church, but he also owned his own hardware and lumber store. He was a giant of a man, with a baritone voice, a quick smile and good counsel.

Mrs. Robinson was a kind lady in her early fifties who was quite religious, even tempered and business oriented. Together, they had three children. The youngest child was Marie, who was in her mid-20's. Andrew was the middle child who was a few years older than Marie, and Ron, who was in his early thirties.

I made myself like a chameleon and tried to fit in within the new household. Mom was here and gone in a matter of weeks. I was the only student that stayed there full-time.

I spent Christmas with Marie on the third floor where she and her parents occupied. Marie was on holiday from teaching college, she was completing her reports and some other projects. I helped her put the finishing touches to her work by drawing maps, food dishes, fruits, and anything else she requested of me. When I was not with Marie I was with Mrs. Robinson at the hardware store, which was located in another part of the parish. I was usually reading, conversing or doing some odd chore which was never too much trouble. I did the best I could to fit in, I spoke when I was spoken to, kept my head in my journal, and completed whatever chores were assigned to me. Basically, I was preparing for school. I cleaned my shorts, assorted my books in my closet, prepared my uniform and of course my church clothes. We attended church approximately three times a week: Sunday, Wednesday and sometimes Friday when they had their "revivals."

Andrew and I had little interaction. So that was my introduction to my family of sorts. Come late December, I was introduced to my fellow borders. First there was a kid named Waylon. He was 16 years old, lanky and very intelligent. He was a sports fanatic, especially anything having to do with the L.A. Lakers. He was in grade 10 and the trendsetter of our dorm, if you could call it that. Next was a kid named Ronish. He was in grade 8, like myself, thirteen years of age, smart, adventurous, studious and had a huge appetite. He was also highly competitive. Genkis was all of the above, with the addition of a bad temper. He was also in grade 8. There was also Triston, the all-around fellow. If he participated, he was efficient, competent, and at the top. He was a very religious person and listened only to gospel music. He would crack jokes, play basketball and study. Finally there were the girls. There were three girls, off the bat I can only specifically remember Sasha, reason being she lived on the other side of the island in Montego Bay and stayed over with me a few weekends. The other two I do not recall their names or where their families lived.

"Simmo" as Waylon was known, sort of looked out for me to an extent. He was said to have a bad effect on me. "If you keep following Waylon" I would always here. I would hear that statement repeated over and over in the intervening months.

Returning to school I fit right back into my little niche. Much had not changed. My old friends were still there, a few new teachers, but still the "same old, same old." I talked more and worked less and the complaints followed. With regular frequency, "Mr. Malvo has a lot of potential, if he could only stop talking and settles down." I spent more time looking from the outside than doing introspection. Looking at me from afar, you would think I was an average kid, just a little on the hyper side, but from a normal family setting.

But soon the trouble began. I altogether stopped doing my laundry, I would not complete my chores and my side of the room (which I shared with Waylon) was a mess. It was entirely because of me. Everyone would leave on Friday and return Sunday; and my dirty clothes would still be in the laundry buckets. I rushed off my assignments and didn't keep up with my shoes, socks, or undergarments. All of my things were scrambled about the room. Everything was all amuck in my life. Come Monday morning I could not even locate my school books. "Oh, well" was my attitude. And being that I did not regularly tend to my laundry, my shoes and clothes were dirty and at school it appeared that I hadn't washed my things in months. I would press my uniform, well...at least my shirt, before school but that was about it.

My grades began to reflect my work ethic. I became the laughing stock, the "dunce" in the group. I held A's and B's on assignments, C's and D's on my tests because I was too busy talking when I should have been studying. I was either drawing or chatting away.

When I was left alone on most weekends, I snuck out. My instructions were to complete my assignments, study, do my laundry and prepare for church. Come Sunday morning I would be ironing a wet church shirt and unable to find a tie or two socks of the same color.

I usually got a speech from Mrs. Robinson, "You know I am going to complain to your mother, and you know she does not play." When my behavior got worse, there were a few threats of an ass-whooping at her hand. She never got around to doing it, though.

Being that I had become the laughing stock and the butt of all jokes, I decided that it may be best to get away from it all. After school I would hitch a ride downtown to see my friends and play a few video games. I thought I might even go to the library in order to write in my journal and get some homework done. I would make it back home just in time before Mr. and Mrs. Robinson arrived.

At the dinner table there would be snickers about my underpants being somewhere in the yard. Oh yeah, the tenants on the first floor complained about my clothes being all over their doorstep. When everyone left on the weekends, the second floor was a mess. I usually got around to cleaning up half the mess. Well, mom called every Friday, which was one thing I could count on. I stood in the office and listened to the barrage for a good forty minutes, praying she didn't have two thirty-minute calling cards.

"You have not written, you missed my birthday, you are so worthless. Didn't I teach you better than that?" On and on, "Don't let me leave to come down there and straighten you out!" My reply was always, "Yes, ma'am." Her response, "You are only saying that, that's all you ever say, goes through one ear and out the other."

I was in the middle of my semester when the money stopped coming. At first, Mrs. Robinson didn't tell me for a month or so. Then one day she sat me down and told me the situation. Nevertheless, she still gave me lunch money and everything seemed the same way as before.

We started a savings system of sorts. Each person paid a certain amount for a hand, one could take as many hands as one could afford and pay the debt off in a year. Every weekend one member got a large sum, in this case, $1,700.00. They would eventually repay in the coming weeks, or rather a year. I took three hands. My numbers were 3, 11 and 89. Each boarder participated and everyone had 3-4 hands. When my week came around, I did some shopping for necessities. I bought a much needed pair of school shoes, a backpack, some socks, a few boxes of saltines and a case or two of sardines.

When all that was done I had about $500 in hand. That Friday, as usual, my mates were picked up one by one by their parents. I would usually not be around, finding some corner to sit in until it hit 6:00pm and everyone was gone. Then I would go upstairs to eat.

Well, one Saturday morning in mid-April, I got a good idea; rather an idea I had the night before. Knowing their usual schedule; and nobody was home but me, I was out of the house, rollerblading, rather circumnavigating the usual route. Mrs. Robinson had already set up a few lookouts for me predicting an escapade into town. I was on the bus to Kingston by 6:30am. I arrived at Curnation Park, smack in the middle of downtown Kingston at about 8:30am. I then took a bus to Aglipark Road, then another to Oakland Road. I got off the bus and headed down the main street to see my father. He saw me coming and met me. He brought me back to the table of dominoes where he and his buddies had been playing. This is where they drank beer or won and lost money on horse races. I told him I was in high school now, my second year, I was boarded out and that mom was in St. Maarten. I could not find the courage to tell him my real intent, I needed somewhere to live, and I had no one else to turn to at the moment. I was hoping he would be able to get my message through my eyes, the way he used to do. However, to my disappointment he gave me a few dollars and sent me packing. He didn't really say what I had expected; obviously he had no intention of keeping me, as he had shouted into the phone two years earlier when mom asked if he would keep me. I had to be back before 6:00pm.

I walked away; my father didn't even get up to walk me to the bus stop. I guess the demands of his game were too important and pressing. A few hundred yards or so, I stopped, leaned on the stop sign, and started crying. An old lady asked, "What's wrong son?" I looked at her, shook my head, and kept on moving.

I was at the Robinson's just in time, in fact, they arrived before me. I had prepared for this. "Where were you?" I see you were off playing basketball. How many times have I told you Lee? We will not be keeping you next semester, your mother has not sent any money and still you will not listen."

I went inside, threw away my dinner, threw my journal into the corner and turned off the lights. I crumpled and cried for a few hours. Then I decided that this would be the last time I did this, as tears do not solve your problems. The holidays quickly came around and mom went to school to collect my grade reports, listen to my teachers and I mean all of them. They all seemed to complain that, "Mr. Malvo's work ethic is poor." Although some of this was true, I was still at the top of my class in the sciences. The semester preceding this one I was first in my class with an average of 92%, but that was with Simone. This was the best I had done since entering high school. I was soon to find out that I had placed 22nd out of 54 students, with an average of 68.5%. This was the worst I had ever done in any school at any point in my life. From the look in my mom's eyes, I could tell she wanted to reach out and strangle me. She stared and Mrs. Robinson and glared at me as well. The only thing that restrained my mom was the fact that Mrs. Robinson was standing beside me, giving her report on my behavior.

Mom explained that she had been detained for "visa fraud" and she lost a lot of money, had been beaten, and her passports were taken. To top it all off, Mrs. Robinson said, "Why don't you stroll downstairs and see his handiwork?" Mom returned with a few torn textbooks that were found along with some underwear that was on my neighbor's doorstep. There was also a bucket full of mildewed uniforms that I never got around to washing. The pile of dishes that had accumulated over the last week were not washed and put away. Mom actually made a list of each and every thing she found, a list for which I would be severely punished.

When she returned, Mrs. Robinson made it very clear. "Ms. James, you will have to find another place to house this young man. We can no longer take him." Quickly, she dragged me by the ear as we went downstairs. She packed up all my stuff while slapping, punching, and cursing at me for hours. Mom gave me all three bags of my belongings that were not thrown in the laundry (a few buckets of mildewed clothes, dog-eared books, and my sketch pads). We left and headed for the bus. We switched buses until we reached "Uncle Dudley's" place. On entering the premises we both heard, "Ms. James, Ms. James, I am so glad to see you." His face, mind you, told a completely different story. "You will have to move, and I mean move as soon as possible. Although you have been a good tenant, that was before you allowed that mad woman to occupy your apartment. She made gifts out of your silverware, stereo system and china and gave it to all her church friends. The woman is crazy, I mean crazy!"

Chapter 7: The Attempt at Suicide

Well, old Dudley's place was a wreck. If something wasn't complete broken it was scratched to hell and back. It was just me and my mom as we stood and surveyed the damage. Of course her frustration turned on me as she began with the usual, extended, lecture. I had sat down in a chair in the corner of the room. A belt and broom stick were close at hand. One by one she rambles off my wrongs, bending one finger back after another to keep count and make sure that I kept count as well. The more she went on the more aggravated she became and then out of nowhere; *"Whap!"* Just like that the blows came raining in – mid sentence – it was as if she had ten hands. It really didn't matter where the blows connected, just that they connected. I was cornered and she left me with welts from head to toe, a swollen left ear and black and blue spots on my ribs. As the days went along, she would leave in search of a new apartment. Finding none, she would return home and the frequency and intensity of the beatings worsened. She became more incensed with my grandmother's antics, who when confronted lied and tried to pick a fight with her (physically). Then she began preaching to my mother how it was, "Una's sins brought her all this trouble. God is telling you something Una." My mom replied with, "Mama, I don't want to hear this; you mean everyone is lying about you and your craziness? You didn't break the microwave? What about that refrigerator? What about the broken sewing machines?"

Mom was enflamed about losing her money and getting deported, she talked about it all day. When I slipped up, which was about twice a day, I got punched, slapped and yelled at. My list of mischievous deeds while she was away didn't help. "You steal, lie and are completely worthless. You have no ambition, just like your father. Not only are you a disgrace, sometimes I wonder if you are even my child." She went on, "I go away for seven months and you carry on."

"Lee, set the table for breakfast!" "Yes, mama," I'd reply. "Lee come here, is this how I taught you....? Answer me!" Slap! Across my face and then blows would begin again.

"Lee, I am going out, mop the house and dust the cabinets." Click! She returns in a few hours and begins to inspect my handiwork. "Lee!" I knew what was coming next.

About two years prior, in 1994 or so, my mom had purchased a quarter acre of land. Now that she couldn't find any apartments, she decided to build a house.

Before actually building a house, she purchased another half-acre on a good deal, or rather a steal. The owner was drunk and she fed him more liquor and bought the title. When the fellow was sober, he didn't care. She found a contractor from the area and began buying lumber, cement and all the other materials. We went to Kingston and bought lots of flowers, chicken, beets, and some non-perishable food for all the workers.

One morning my grandmother decided that she wanted to preach to me. It was about 11:00am and I told her that "I don't want to hear this!" I then went back to bed. Grandma cornered me later in the day and gave me a stern lecture about respect and then attempts to beat me with her fists. Mom stopped her and told her to leave. "But Una..." Mom said to me, "I don't care, you won't listen, just leave! There are your clothes, out, out the door; I can't deal with you right now."

Later we both (mom and I) walked to the construction site. I sometimes worked as a laborer; she chipped in just as hard if not harder than everyone else. After returning from the site, she usually got in an argument with Dudley (the landlord). All of a sudden he says, "I hear you are building yourself a house, good, good! I am increasing your rent!" "What?" Mom replied. And thus yet another argument started.

Most days, for some reason or another, I got whooped. One day, after having a heated argument with Ms. Allen, the old hag who lived with Uncle Dudley, mom returned. She had told me to wash the dishes. I was tired and had forgotten, and by that I mean that I had completely dozed off on the porch and left the door wide open. She returned and got around to seeing unwashed dishes. My sleep was interrupted by a prompt smack across my head. I was still shaking the cobwebs off of me when I heard, "Get up! Go do the dishes you lazy ass." She had blocked my way to the kitchen as she continued; "I go away, work three jobs and come home to nothing but bad reports." I mutter some excuses, frowning. "You had better get that look off your face, you hear me?" I grunt some more under my breath, then she spun me around and began punching.

I escaped the blows by running out of the house. I returned from Dudley's mango walk (a few hundred acres of mango trees) and went into the back yard. It was dark by then and the carpentry shop next to the house was closing. "Blacka," a fellow that worked there, was closing and the last person to leave. He saw me plotting something and said, "What are you doing Lee?" "I am fine." I replied. I then found a tall tree really close by. I made a knot from a rope fashioned out of sheets. I tested its strength, and then placed it around my neck. I tightened the slack, sat on the limb while shaking and crying. I yelled my mother's name as loud as I could. She comes out to the summons of my voice and I told her to stop right where she was standing. "Stay at that distance." I said. As I formed my reasoning, I will save her all the trouble. "You won't have to beat me anymore!" She and Blacka spent four hours trying to talk me out of it. My mom continues to talk as Blacka disappears. In a few minutes, he reappears under the tree. Angered by his decision to move beneath the tree I jump! As I await the rope to tighten and snap my neck, I feel his hands grab me. Blacka pulls me up, takes the rope off my neck and brings me safely down. Mom runs to my side, taking me into the house. This was the first time I saw a pale black woman. That is how her face looked, completely devoid of blood. My eyes were blood shot from nearly being strangled to death, and mom began to cry. She gave me some lecture about fear; I cannot to this day remember her exact words. It is pretty much a blank in my mind.

The next morning she awoke before me, I packed my cooler and grabbed the bags with the workmen's tools. She tells me to just stay home. She returned around 4:00pm that evening, complaining that the men were cheating her out of her money. The construction is not where it was supposed to be by this time. Mom said, "They told me it would be roofed by now, we're still blocking up the walls, and then the wall in the hallway upstairs just fell down. How the hell does a wall fall down? I fired Rasco (one of the workers), that idiot didn't fit the corner beams properly, so I have to buy all of them again." Although her frustration, at first, was not directed at me, there was one problem. I had been home all day and the house was just the way it was when she left. So guess what, her frustration then shifts towards me, grandma, the deportation, and then back to me again. "You.....you are the worst problem in my life. If, if it weren't for you, me and Maglo (her estranged husband) would still be together. But it is you, you and all your problems!"

The scenario was different, but the script was always the same. I got an ass –whooping. She opens the door and says, "Go on! Go on and kill yourself. It would be cheaper burying your ass than living with you. You ain't nothing but a waste of my time and money." She went on, "Why don't you go hang yourself?" She urged me to kill myself some more. I just walked away and meditated on all her words. I returned and slept in the chair inside the dining hall, or rather spent all night going over my life, stage after stage, year after year.

I tied a couple of pieces of rope together and really thought about committing suicide again. I'd just had enough of my life. For some reason, I had lost the courage. I just couldn't do it. After that I pretty much kept to myself. When my mom was in the right mood she would hug me and ask, "Are you ok? Why won't you talk?" Then two hours later I was the worst thing that happened to the world since 1985. Simple conversation ended up with me in pain because I didn't answer her in time. Sometimes I didn't know the reason. Such was the inconsistency of our relationship, with me being the punching bag to release her stress.

I was relieved to see my Aunt Marie, a temporary break, or at least a distraction for my mom. If I could make myself as unobtrusive as possible, maybe, just maybe, I could get a week or so of respite. But of course I was to be disappointed. Aunt Marie had arrived at mom's request to discuss sharing the burden of their mother. Mary had kept her for the last few years. They agreed that Aunt Marie would keep grandma and mom would help pay her doctor bills. They went shopping together and bought several pounds of fish and all sorts of vegetables and spices. Upon their return, we all went to work cleaning and seasoning the fish. The following morning I awoke to the sound of frying and laughing. For once they sounded like sisters reminiscing about their horrible pasts, laughing at it all. As usual, peace was not to be long-lived. Carlene, Stacy and I got the dishes ready. I ate some peppermint and we made some tea. We set chairs in a small paved area in front of the house. We, as children, sat at the steps, waiting for orders to go fetch this or that.

Everyone was eating and the conversation turns our way, the three ungrateful rascals. My mother and aunt began a heated debate about how useless and ungrateful we all were, and how we had so much versus their fatherless upbringing, etc., etc. As I listened to it all, I recall thinking that these people must be insane! The more they talked, the angrier I got. I was subjected to unpleasant stares and finger pointing for several minutes. Mom begins to talk about how disgusted she is of me and my "boarding adventures," and how the Robinson's said, "We will not keep him under any circumstance." Marie adds, "He just won't listen, that is why I told you I would not keep him another year."

I wanted so badly to shout what was on my mind. Had I spoke it would have gone something like this; "We didn't ask to come here, you had us, why didn't you give us away, and we might have turned out better." I stifled the thought and banished it from my mind, or at least I thought so. I am called to clear the dishes from the small center table. "Get that!" "Why is it that you can't do anything right?" My usual response was "Yes, ma'am," only this time a little slip of the tongue and I answered, "Like I asked to come here, it's always me." A quick look from my mom and a slap across the mouth was my instant reward. As usual, I didn't see the hand coming; just felt the sting across my face. I was banished for the day into the kitchen to wash the mountain of dishes, pots, pans, utensils and other assorted items. I grumbled to myself and my progress was quite slow, the more I worked, the more the dishes seemed to pile up. I had just received a "fresh batch." My mom didn't tolerate the smallest form of grumbling from me because she was the "perfect parent."

Using my peripheral vision, I could see a shadow approaching and dropped the plate that was in my hands. The kitchen door closes as I assumed the worst. To my surprise it was Carlene bringing yet another batch of dishes. She saw the look on my face and smiled. She helped me sweep up the broken pieces and started to tell me to hurry up, "If you organize like this it will go faster," then she told me to watch her do it. She sped through the whole pile in a few minutes. I tried Carlene's way which actually worked quite well, until the next batch arrived. Stacy dropped them off without offering a glance in my direction. I was the new "plague," or so it seemed. Refocusing on the task at hand I worked slowly and ran through my mental list of all the things I was going to tell my mother when I was older and on my own. I suddenly felt a presence behind me but by then it was too late. I felt the first pain across my back. I lifted my hands to shield or at least deflect some of the blows. I hear the scream, "Lord, Jesus!" I turned around, I heard footsteps retreating and hear more yelling, "Lord, Jesus! Lord, Jesus!" I looked at the floor and I saw the blood, lots of it. I started trembling. "She is going to kill me; I grabbed a grocery bag, packed some fried fish and bread and decided against going into the bedroom to get some clothes and I dashed off.

For a little over a day I stayed out in the mango walk, watching the house, trying to figure out what I was going to do. It was nighttime and the kitchen door was open, so I decided to chance sneaking in and getting my clothes and some more food. As soon as I set foot inside the darkness, I was snatched off my feet, the door was slammed and I heard the snarl, "If I put my hands on you, they're going to charge me for murder!" I am shoved into the dining room, mom stands there for about twenty minutes shaking and twitching, all the while staring me in my eyes. Then she exhaled, walked away and returned with two stools. She sat them atop one another, "Step on the chair and get on top of the stools!" I followed her orders. She demands, "Hold your hands in front of you, and you better not drop them!" Eight hours later she returns and tells me to put my hands down. She then directs, "Now stand on your right leg, using your right hand to hold your left ear." My left hand was also directed to hold my right leg. She told me to change into various positions for two and a half days. Whenever my stance would falter, I needed to use the bathroom or sleep, she returned to the door, the look in her eyes, her hand still clenched in a fist. I forgot all about sleep or food. During the third day she asked me if I needed to apologize. I did reluctantly. I would pay for my reluctance.

The following day I sat in a corner of the kitchen, I knew that the punishment was coming; it was just a matter of time. I sat there and began to cry. She enters the kitchen and hears my sobbing. "I want you to stop crying, so shut up." ...... "Shut up Lee!" ..... "I will give you something to cry for, you hear me, and I said shut up!"

I made my best attempt to stop the tears, but they kept coming. When I looked up she had started to become agitated again as she began to shake and turn red. This made me sob all over again. First she hollered, "I said shut up!" I am met with a slap across the face. "Shut up I tell you!" Then she begins listing her grievances, started from years ago, and the blows kept coming. "This is for you, you did it on purpose!" The last act of defiance must have stepped up the punishment a notch because now there were no slaps, only punches.

When it was all said and done my hollering and whining did nothing. No one came to my aid. My head was left with two scars, welts from head to toe along with two dislocated fingers on my right hand (index and middle finger). This was the second time my middle finger had popped out of its socket from one of mom's beatings. And just like before I closed my eyes and pop both joints back into place. It hurt like hell, but then again I was in pain all over.

Have you ever been beaten so badly that you could not sit, sleep, or eat? It was like being stomped by a bunch of bullies three times your size.

The house was not coming along well and remained unfinished. Mom decided that she had to travel again to some small island. The only place I could return to was back to Pearla's.

Chapter 8: The Return to Pearla!

Mom asked Sonia (Pearla) if she would allow me to stay there again. She said, "Yes, but he should never have left in the first place." I was thinking to myself that if I did well during this semester that mom would just stay home. Better still, I would talk to the principal and my guidance counselor about my situation. I explained my position to them, alluding to the violence without saying as much, and that it would be in my best interest if my mother stayed home. While I did not get an answer one way or another, at least I put the information out there.

Mom would come on her regular visits to see how well I was doing. We met with my guidance counselor and I explained again why I think it was important that she stayed home. The guidance counselor sided with my mother, who insisted that she must travel because she was the sole provider. I retorted quickly that she could sew and open up a shop, and that she had enough money left over to do that. She looked at me angrily and says she is buying a ticket to try yet another small island (to gain access to the United States).

We then go to the vice principal's office who sides with me saying, "Ms. James, the child needs a stable home somewhere to settle down, he cannot keep rolling from place to place. This is doing him no good. You have an intelligent son who can do well if he has a steady support system."

This, of course, fell on mother's deaf ears. We walked out of the office and I said to her, "Don't you see that you are losing me, can't you see it?" I walked off. What was she going to do, punch me in the mouth in front of all the other parents seated or stand in the hallway?

Mom asked me the following evening if I knew anyone who I could buy my text books from through a second-hand source. I told her that I did. I was thinking that Waylon would give the books to me and I will use the money to repay my debt, so everyone wins.

So I told mom that I needed $1,300.00 to pay my friend for the books, as that was what he was asking. I asked Waylon for the text books and he gave them to me. He then brought up my debt – as in when I was going to pay him. I smiled and handed him all the cash.

Mom returned two weeks later and I had all my text books with the exception of two. I told her I was offered the books from some of my friends. I told her that they were allowing me to keep the books for the entire school year. I went to school thinking that everything was fine. When I returned home that evening to my surprise my mom was still there. While she gave me a hug and welcomed me, as soon as I was inside the house the door slams and the windows were closed. I was thinking to myself, "Oh no, she's found out about the debt with Summo." I was wrong. With an air of indignation, she holds in her hand my correspondence with Kedian, my girlfriend. This included several cards and gifts. I looked at the box where I had made slits and dropped the letters inside the cardboard thinking that surely no one would ever think to look there. It had worked for three years and as the saying goes, "All good things must come to an end." And what an end this would be. She started going through the letters one by one. Reading along Kedian's words to me, "So you think I am spending my money on some no good, two-bit…you never sent me one card, not even one Valentine's Day or birthday card in three years, how many cards did you buy her?"

I looked back at her with disgust. One verbal slip, "What, you expected me to be a faggot!" Mom responded to this comment with a "Whap!" She looked at the belt, grabbed it and started to hit me. I looked at her and decided I would not cry or holler no matter how bad this beating was going to be. She said, "Oh, so you think you are a man now, grown up and tough, so want a fight?" I stood there and stared her down. She look again at the belt, smiled, threw it at the bed and started punching. I lifted my hand, weaving to block the blows; this only brought out more rage. I mean the woman lost it and went into some crazy frenzy.

Pearla came up from her shop and began banging on the door, "Una! Una! Jesus Christ, you are going to kill him!" She got the door open and pulled my mother off of me. I was on the ground; she had gotten on my back and sat down on me. Using the same leather belt that she carried around for these occasions and beat whatever it was that she was screaming about out of me. I do not remember getting up because I had been knocked out. I do remember waking up in the morning and hearing Pearla telling my mother, "Una! Una! You can't beat him no more. I heard that boy hollering all the way down in my shop." She went on, "Una, when you get mad, you get so angry you could kill him!"

Pearla accompanied her to another room to keep me safe from her going absolutely bezerk. Out of nowhere I heard, "Who is she? Get up, you are going to school and you're going to show her to me." I replied, "No.!" She grabbed at me but Pearla pushed her outside saying, "Una, I will talk to him."

Pearla returns inside, "Lee, you know your mother is mad at you and will do nothing short of murdering you to find out who she is. If you don't tell her she is still going to find out one way or the other, so just make it easy on yourself and tell her." I nodded in the affirmative. For two days, I rested in bed and healed my wounds. I had to lie on my stomach because my back felt broken and was black and blue. I could not sit down, my hands were swollen and my ribs hurt (though I didn't think anything was broken). The only place untouched was my head.

I got dressed and headed to school. A few days had passed and my mom had yet to make an appearance there. One day, the following week, she pops in unexpectedly. I saw her talking to my homeroom teacher, Ms. Maxwell. I was called out of class; she still had that "I am going to kill you" look on her face. "Lee, you lied to me. I asked Waylon and he said he gave you the books for free!" Ms. Maxwell looked at me. "Lee, your mother asked me about Kedian and I told her I knew the two of you were good friends but that the relationship was not harmful."

Mom moved forward with her plans and left for Antigua two weeks later. She arranged to send my lunch money directly to my teacher and I was to eat in the classroom. That was her way of making sure that none of her money touched my hands. It also guaranteed that I could buy no gifts for Kedian. It was a pity she did not know that I had developed into a miser. I saved 90% of my lunch money, which would come in handy later on. In a month or so the lunch money had completely stopped. She also stopped paying for Sonia, who in turn neglected me because I would not listen. She grew tired of beating me because I would arrive home just a little later each evening. Ms. Maxwell realized that although I was being cared for and attending school, I looked and like a bag of rags. Teachers, for a change, had not complained about my mouth in months. I didn't venture to the volleyball or basketball court, just sat in my little corner and chilled out by myself. A few friends tried to cheer me up, but it didn't work. *This is where I think the change took place or at the very least, started.* I began to withdraw from the world. Ms. Maxwell noted the change in my behavior and decided to take me into her home.

Chapter 9: The Maxwell's

I had been maturing a little but the thought was hitting home that I better start acting right. Being 15, I would be on my own in three years, tops, if I was lucky.

At the Maxwell's I was given my own room. I just became part of the family; they treated me as if I had always been there. I talked a lot less, did my work, attended school and put forth a greater effort academically. I jumped up on the school's ratings board from 16th to 9th.

Mr. Maxwell and I hit it off from the start. We talked about almost everything. On weekends we spent our days on the farm. I was given my own little plot of land. I planted cabbage, carrots and bell peppers. It was great. It was a rewarding feeling to see the plants come to life.

When I wasn't checking my seedlings, I was on the river investigating bugs and plants. If I was not doing that, I was down the street, hanging out with a few classmates, just having fun.

I helped as much as I could, Mr. Maxwell's sister had a little bar and shop. I would help out there on weekends, sit behind the counter and do my homework, even serve up a few red stripe beers.

At the end of the term I looked at my commendations (grades). I had A's, B's, and 2 C's, which was not too bad. "I will get straight A's next semester" I remember saying to myself. While standing in the school's auditorium one day, just observing the stage, I thought that when I walk off across that stage I will have really earned my diploma. It was a good feeling. I had been placed in all the classes I needed to pursue for a career as an aviator. The classes included chemistry, physics, biology, geometry among a list of business subjects. In mid-August, while enjoying the holidays, my mother called and informed Mrs. Maxwell that I will be immigration to Antigua to live with her. She was told to take me to the airport on a certain date. I had conflicting feelings on whether or not I wanted to go be with my mother or not. I didn't want to leave the Maxwell's farm. For once the future wasn't looking all that bad after all. Mrs. Maxwell saw that I didn't want to leave. While packing, I looked across the bed and just shook my head. She came over and hugged me. "I know Lee, you don't want to go, but she is your mother, I have to send you."

Chapter 10: A Bit Sooner than I Anticipated

I arrived in Antigua in 1999. I settled in a small one room apartment without bathroom facilities. Mom was a self-employed peddler on Queen Elizabeth highway, just a few blocks from my new school. In my mind I didn't want to confront my feelings about my mother or towards my past, but I saw it necessary to just move on beyond them and go along with the flow. For the remainder of the summer holidays, I helped my mother peddling during the carnival festivities. I was mobile and moved along with the crowds; selling jerk chicken, snacks, drinks and liquor. We made barely enough to eat and pay rent. Most of my tuition came from my mother's boyfriend, Mr. Williams. He was quite a man. He was about 62 years old at the time, tall at about 6'4" and a constant prankster. He just loved practical jokes and was a laid back kind of fellow, always smiling. He was a bit on the slim side, with a receding hairline and a little salt and pepper look to his hair. His clothes were always simple – slacks, sneakers and t-shirt. I disliked the entire affair but was in no position to alter the circumstances.   When I mentioned my displeasures to my mother, she said, "I was throwing things in her face."

At school I didn't fit in at first. I was external, insecure, talkative, and often caused the class to have extra homework. As a bustling high school sophomore, I was the kid who had his hand up for every question.   The school was a small private Christian institution and my class was small with just 33 students. The main difference in comparison to my other schools was the quality of the teaching staff. Their teaching style was much more engaging. They were actually interested in the feedback, quick to correct, slow to scold and the work was well-structured. Students knew exactly what the semester's objective was and how we were going to go about achieving our goals. Dr. Aaron was our modestly dressed, abrasive in style, mostly serious, far from wishy-washy, adventurous teacher. On occasion, she could be affable when she decided the particular situation called for it. I quickly caught on to the various nicknames she had earned over the years.

Personally, with having mother around I had to give her money's worth or I would surely hear, "I promise I will stop wasting my money!" She destroyed my address book and divested me of my pre-paid phone card. That pretty much ended the ability to keep up with Kedian. I decide to focus on the essential subjects, study the nuances. I liked information technology, computers and various business subjects. I was again labeled a "chatterbox." However, the teachers saw some potential so that actually gave me some leverage. I decided that I needed more than geometry to have any chance at aeronautical engineering. My math teacher, Mrs. Nicholas, managed to make math interesting. This was the only class that got my complete and undivided attention. She punctuated the important points in the lesson, gave you at least three easier ways to approach the problem, explained the step-by-step procedures to problem solving and had a very simple, but effective work ethic. On the other hand, her husband, Mr. Nicholas was different. I will be as objective as possible in my description. He was a great teacher in that he understood the material. He knew how to present history and social studies in a format that students could retain and enjoy. However, he was a complete control freak and authoritarian. He was aggressive towards me and I couldn't allow my ego to submit and lose face before my peers. I was the overcompensating odd ball in his classroom. The student that got a "talking to" all day, yet answered 90% of the questions being asked of me, somehow still falling short. An example would be, "Mr. Malvo, now that you bring that up, I should make that as assignment for all the students." Then I would try to talk my way out of trouble, only digging myself even deeper.

Within four months of immigrating to Antigua, I was left completely on my own. In January 2000, mom decided she was going to visit St. Maarten to try her luck once again at gaining entry into the United States. She knew and could still reach some of the contacts when she got her visa the first time. This time, she intended to try to be smuggled in on boats into St. Thomas. The Christmas semester had ended; mom had paid $400 towards the January to March semester and two months' rent. As soon as she left, I used the little savings I had to buy a second-hand computer, stole a few zip drives and a CD/DVD burner. My first scramble was stealing the latest CD's, then making copies and reselling them at a much lower price. I did the very same with the latest DVD's, though they didn't sell much. From there I stole a CD player, calculator, you name it. If someone (a customer) wanted a video game, computer software or anything that I could resell, I stole it. I told them to give me three days and I would have it for them and I usually did. My most dependable catch was the church offering plate. On a good weekend the church plate yielded between $75 and $100 EC (Eastern Caribbean currency). The exchange rate at the time was $1.00 U.S. equaled $2.20 EC. Two months flew by fast and I had enough for the rent which was $400. Mr. Williams came by every two weeks and gave me $50.00, so that helped me pay the light bill.

Most of my remaining money came from stealing art products such as paint, pencils, sketch pads, brushes, etc. Most of my customers were outside of my school. The only thing my classmates knew was that Lee attended school, did his work and seemed normal. A month went by and rent again was due along with my tuition. I stole a few watches and gold chains from the mall. I stole three Timex watches and some really cheap gold chains that put the rent in my pocket and enough to pay for the electricity. But still, no school fee. A friend (Ravel) and I would hang out on Friday around the mall and a video game arcade. We attended private school so we were looked at as potential thieves. Ravel, by the way, always had money.

I would use some of his money to buy a few cheap CD's, and then stole four new ones. At the arcade I would steal some of the latest PlayStation games of which sold pretty easily. Well, we were in the island's largest bookstore and this is where I found my lucky break. Ravel was buying a few supplies for the technical drawing class. The man behind the cash register was counting money. Ravel asked him for a scientific calculator, he replied that the calculators were not on the shelf because he just got them in. He placed the money bag behind the register. I told Ravel to grab a pack of pencils, no sooner as he leaves the counter I reached over and grabbed the bag, removed the money that was already counted and wrapped it in a rubber band and moved out. I hit the door, the cashier was not yet back at the cash register, and the line had just built up to about seven or eight customers. My catch was $2,300.00. I paid two months' rent, stocked up on four cases of ramen soup, lentil beans and two boxes of chicken back. I also bought two or three cases of cheap saltines, a few cases of sardines and a case of corned beef. By Monday morning I had $1,000.00 still left in my hand. I paid $400.00 for that semester. I bought season tickets to cricket matches which Ravel and I attended after school. We were joined on weekends by John, a good friend and classmate, and a cricket "fanatic." I had blown $350.00 in three weeks or so, which left me with $250.00 in my hand. I put down this amount as savings for next semester. This provided a much needed break because the island only had 60,000 residents; essentially you can only steal from so many stores.

From there on out, which was about May 2000, I sold about twelve CD's a week which gave me $60.00 or so. When I was at church the opportunity shared itself again and I got about $75.00. This amount, along with selling a few CD players and two pocket game boys provided me with enough until June's tuition was due. Only $400.00 of the $600.00 of course, so I owed them an additional $200.00. I had gotten into two fights over my money. The first was at a basketball court because this dude owed me $50.00 and kept stalling. I came out with a swollen eye, and he was left with a few swells of his own. I applied some ice to my eye and by Monday morning I was pretty much as good as new. The second fight was over some computer simulation games. I met a kid after school, Charles was his name. He was about 6' even and 175 lbs. I was about 5'5" and 125 lbs. He did not know how to use his body weight but he hit hard. I bobbed and weaved most of his blows, and I landed most. All said and done, he caught me with a good shot and "aired me out." That was all she wrote. I remember being tapped on my chin of glass, dazed, blinking, I saw him coming and it seemed like three of him. He moved to my right, I staggered to the left and tried to block with my right hand. I was rewarded with a nice volley from the left under and up, to the left side of my head. The rest is history. So there went $75.00. You win some and you lose some right? He got a coke bottle (glass) to the head two days later and I had been ditching my old path home ever since. The dude from the basketball court did eventually pay up, and then cheated me out of some more money. This time he had a few friends with him and me being alone and a stranger to the island, what was $40.00, right?

The end of June had come and it was rent time again, so I started to ditch my landlord Elmore. He was a very kind person and to that I owe him for not throwing me out on the street. I hung out after school at the library and did my homework. I left the house at about 5:20am or so, but no later. My food was down to a few cases of lentil beans, sugar and 20 pounds of flower. I had $100.00 in my pocket. The lights got cut off as I was unable to pay the bill. My wardrobe consisted of three shirts and three pairs of pants. I mostly wore my yellow t-shirt (for my house color) which was part of the school dress code. I washed my pants and hand pressed them immediately after removing them from the clothes line. Some school days I stayed at another classmate's house. I would carry my uniform in my bag. I also slept in an abandoned house which was right beside the main street and next to a street light. I spent my nights under a blanket, using the street light to study. I went home between July and early August to cook some beans, wash my clothes and that was pretty much it. Elmore couldn't catch up with me because I wasn't there. By the way, I had destroyed the interior walls of the shack with my fists; it was really just a one room with plywood and an outside toilet with sewer water running right along the back of the house. The grass was packed with garbage and when the rain fell it would always flood and the mixture was like goulash.

I did fine on my final exams in July and I made the honor roll with an 87%. In my way of looking at things, that wasn't bad with all things considered. During my final days on the island is when I first saw John Allen Muhammad. He was at Zaza's Electronic and Computer Repair Shop, where a few kids played computer games. Mr. Muhammad's son, John Jr., was playing a flight simulator game. I watched the relationship they had. He was talking to his son to return to the cockpit view, saying, "You don't fly a plane from the inside out." John Jr. laughed and returned to his instrument panel. He then went on to practice as his father had recommended, with just the instrument panel by island hopping in a thunderstorm. There was so much laughter, joking and encouragement. It was just something I was not used to seeing between a father and his son.

Chapter 11: Cementing My Trust

At the end of July 2000 my mother sent me a plane ticket so that I could join her in St. Maarten. Seven months before our reunion she had left Antigua for St. Maarten with a goal of entering into the United States. On my arrival I was met at the airport by my mother and a middle-aged Haitian named Jacob.

In 1997, Jacob was responsible for getting my mother documents to enter the United States. He had procured for her a U.S. visa, residence papers, social security number and legitimate identification. My mother and over a dozen other people were arrested in a raid carried out by the immigration authorities of St. Maarten. All the aforementioned documents were seized. Jacob was still in business, my mother and I were supposed to take a boat to the island of St. Thomas, and thus, enter the United States through the U.S. Virgin Islands. I disliked Jacob immediately. My suspicions as to his character were soon confirmed. He had taken my mother's $4,500.00 (U.S. currency) and then strung her beads of lies upon the thread of his twisted tongue for the next nine months. My mother had two big bruises on her arm and forearm when I first arrived. When I questioned her about the bruises she changed the subject. Jacob was callous in manner, verbally and physically abusive and disrespectful towards my mother. He would show up at my mother's apartment to eat her food and make more promises. My mother was very good at spotting a con-man, but her strong desire to go to the United States created a blind spot. Jacob had the contacts and he used this carrot to his advantage. In early August 2000, Jacob moved us in with a Haitian family. The household was made up of two adult siblings, a brother and a sister, both in their late twenties. We were supposed to be on the same boat which would be leaving the following weekend. We all lived in a basement, one room, studio apartment, with my mother and I lodging in the living room. To ensure that we all got along it was agreed upon that we do our share of the chores. Mom decided that we should get out of the house during the day. We visited a family member who had long established residency on the Dutch side of the island.

The deadline for our departure came and went and Jacob never even contacted us to provide an explanation or give an update. When he did show up, two weeks had passed. He spent most of his time conversing with the Haitians in Creole. Jacob and the adult siblings would cast furtive glances at my mother and me during their banter which would be followed by laughter.

My mother had cooked dinner, everyone was served a plate. I didn't eat. I stood in the doorway of the apartment staring at Jacob. Every time my mother brought up the subject of our departure, everyone would look at her out the corner of their eyes and fan her away dismissively. My mother walked past me sighing heavily, dejection and frustration written upon her face as she placed dishes into the kitchen sink. She then returned to the living room and something inside me just gave way. Jacob got a call on his cell phone and excused himself to talk in the privacy of the kitchen. The kitchen was quite small. Jacob was bent over slightly at the waist resting his left elbow on the countertop. While everyone was eating dinner I had made my way into the kitchen. I inspected the knives and choose the meat cleaver I had it hidden behind my back. Jacob was preoccupied when I entered the room, engrossed in his conversation. I had the meat cleaver in the middle of the back of my pants. I closed the apartment door as I had the key in my possession. The basement has no windows for escape. I walked towards Jacob placing a cup in the sink. I quickly stepped towards Jacob, grabbed him by his shirt collar and slammed him into the wall. He was cornered in an area where the trash can was kept between the store and the counters. There was a 90 degree angle where both walls met. The store was on one side of the kitchen, the kitchen counters on the other. Before he could react, I swung the cleaver across my body from left to right aiming for his mid-section. Jacob stepped backwards and I cut his shirt. The slice was followed by an immediate punch to his jaw and a kick to his stomach. From a somewhat crouched position Jacob charged me as I kneed him in the face. I kicked him and he fell backwards. He screamed for my mother saying, "Una, Una, come get your boy!" Jacob curled up into a ball as I proceeded to kick him repeatedly. The cleaver was raised over my head when someone grabbed my right wrist. It was the other young Haitian. To get him off me, I kicked him again in the stomach. Jacob tried to rush me again and I kicked him on the shin, he recoiled backwards and I chopped at his head with the meat cleaver. I missed making a large divot in the concrete wall behind him. By then I was being restrained by my mother and the two siblings. They pulled me into the living room. Jacob ran to the door and found it locked. The young Haitian man had an extra key on his key ring and let him out. My mother was in total shock, she and the others stood between me and the door. I was pacing back and forth, grumbling to myself. My mother pulled me into the kitchen once everyone had left and said, "Lee, what have you done? Why? Why did you attack him?" "Are you blind? He is using you mom! And don't tell me he didn't put his hands on you. All he does is lie. Fuck him! In fact, get dressed we are going down to his brother's house to get all your money back – all of it!" She had never seen me angry and was frozen, still trying to come to grips with what she had just witnessed. I put my boots on and held the door for her. Before we left I apologized to the Haitian siblings. They too had paid their money in advance. I explained my dilemma and that he had physically abused my mother, disrespected her, and I had finally had enough. My mother and I caught the bus to the area where Jacob lived at his brother's house. When we arrived we found four people already gathered before the house, shouting and demanding that Jacob return their money. We joined the crowd. Jacob opened a window and threatened all of us that he had a gun and would not hesitate to use it. I walked off in search of something to throw into his car's windshield. I found a broken cinder block not too far away, grabbed it, and let it fly. I then proceeded to do the same to all the cars. I slashed his tires and banged his car repeatedly with some steel rebar that I had found, denting it wherever I could. I was on the hood of his car, stomping it in. I saw him watching from the window. I identified myself, "This is Lee! Can you see? Can you hear me now? You are a bitch! You are not going to bust a fucking grape! You are not going to shoot shit! Shut the fuck up. I will do to you what I have just done to your car. We have got your house surrounded and we are not leaving. The only way you walk out alive is to bring my mother her money – all of it!" After that, I jumped off the hood of his totaled vehicle and threw a rock at the window where he was standing. The stone connected and broke the window. More and more people began to gather on all sides of the home. Everyone was armed with something and was growing angrier with each passing minute. Jacob's brother finally came out of the house with a cardboard box. He was pleading that we not destroy his residence. He called people by name and paid them. My mother got back $3,700.00 of the $4,500.00, but it was close enough. We then returned to the studio apartment and packed our belongings. I again apologized to the Haitians for disrespecting their home. We found lodging at a relative's house for a further four days.

My mother hatched a plan. She spent $2,500.00 on purchasing clothing, jewelry, make-up, etc. When we returned to Antigua we went from house to house and sold these products. We started off by selling to the people we knew. We sold mostly on credit and collected the remainder of the debts on a weekly basis. We returned in time for me to go back to school. In order for us to remain in Antigua we had to get our permits renewed. It was at the immigration office in St. John's, Antigua where my mother first heard of the "American" who could get people into the United States." This was in October 2000.

My mother had rekindled her relationship with an elderly gentleman named Theodore Williams. She talked him into giving her $50,000.00 EC ($25,000.00 USD). She promised to stay with him if he built her a house and gave her the money needed to start her business. Mr. William's promptly did both and began the construction of a home, giving my mother all the money. Three days after hearing about this "American," we went to meet him. The man who could get legitimate American identification, birth certificates and passports was John Allen Muhammad.

John charged $3,500.00 for the package my mother wanted. My mother and I visited John's residence daily. We were introduced to his three children: John Jr., aged 11, Selena, aged 9, and Taalibah, aged 7. By November 15, 2000, my mother was in the United States. I got very ill several months after my mother left. For the first eight years of my life I had suffered with bouts of rheumatic fever. I had such an attack during this period that I was completely bed-ridden. Muhammad visited to check in on me and found the door open. He took me to the doctor where I received antibiotic shots. Muhammad stayed with me, kept me at his house for nearly a week and nursed me back to health. During this week I told John my life's story, and that I had first seen him at Zaza's Electronic and Computer Repair Shop playing a flight simulator game with his son. Muhammad had saved my life. Once I was well, I moved all my mother's furniture out of the apartment to a storeroom at Mr. Williams' house. Mr. Williams had broken his arm so I stayed with him and helped him out for two or three weeks until his arm was close to being healed. Since my mother had in so many words stolen from Mr. Williams, I was very uncomfortable living with him. Add to this, two of his children (who were around my mother's age) lived not too far from his house. I learned that they hated our guts.

I therefore spent the Christmas holiday week with Muhammad. It was during this period that I asked Mr. Muhammad if I could live with him. He told me that I could. From then on, for three to four weeks, Muhammad took me around and introduced me to his clients, contacts and friends as his son. He taught me the "business" along with precautions he had put into place. In mid-

February 2001, Muhammad was detained in the United States. I got a call from him. I was told to get the children and move them to the "safe house" and if possible, to grab the money. I left school immediately and pulled his children out of their school. I took them to Andrea's house. Andrea was Muhammad's girlfriend that no one knew about but me. When I returned to grab the money, the police raid was already under way. They seized at least $160,000.00 (US Dollars) and $36,000.00 EC (Eastern Caribbean Dollars). I had within my possession a debit card that was in Andrea's name. For the next month, John Junior and I travelled at night. The girls were not allowed to leave the house. I home schooled the children and with Andrea's help, kept everyone sane. I delivered the birth certificates, identification cards, and Antiguan passports to eight clients and I collected their money. I took care of John's children until May 2001. This was a stressful period because I couldn't answer their questions as to when their father would ever return home.

On May 1, 2001 Muhammad returned to Antigua. He brought gifts for everyone. I turned over to him what money I had remaining. I explained that I would have had more of his money but I had to bribe the children by spoiling them in order to keep them preoccupied until his return. The greatest gift I could have ever received was bestowed upon me the first night of his return. Everyone was in bed; I was sitting on the back steps at Andrea's place just staring at the stars when I felt a tap on my shoulder. It was Muhammad. There was a pause as we stared at each other. He pulled me up, hugged me tight and patted me on the back saying, "Great job, son!" During the brief three months we spent together in

Antigua, Muhammad taught me quite a bit. Most of it I absorbed through osmosis from watching him. Muhammad listened and cared about what I had to say. On one occasion in particular, I asked him a question about world history he could not answer. Muhammad had set a date for us to go to the library to find out the answer. If he was wrong, I could correct him without fear of punishment or beatings. Once a week he would take one of his children for a walk. During these two hours you could ask him anything, there were no stupid questions. He never tried to interrogate us and allowed us to tell him whatever we wished. We always arrived at what really mattered to us – in this roundabout way of conversing. I was introduced to the Nation of Islam philosophy at this time. I was also introduced to systematic training in physical fitness. Mr. Muhammad, John junior and I would go on three mile runs four days a week. John junior was given a three minute head start and I was given a two minute head start. Muhammad would try to catch us. Each morning I escaped his grasp by a few inches, but he always caught John junior. After two months of this training and daily calisthenics, he could no longer catch either of us. The teachings of the Nation of Islam inculcated that one should eat a single meal a day, as this is what the prophet Muhammad did. I began eating twice daily with the aim of eventually getting to the point of eating one meal a day in eighteen months.

It was in May 2001 when Muhammad, me, and his three children arrived in the United States. Muhammad had obtained legitimate papers for me to travel with him. I quickly had learned from John, "If parents embodied half of what they preached, they would have half as many problems with their children."

Chapter 12: Running to My Death

I had officially entered the United States with John on May 31, 2001. Later that evening we were picked up by one of John's friends. We were taken to his apartment in Fort Lauderdale. It was there that I spent the first two weeks, most days just babysitting the kids while Muhammad was out on "business." By the third week my mother caught wind of me being there. She contacted Muhammad telling him that she wanted to see her son. "How dare he keep me three weeks without telling her? Haven't you had him long enough? I may be poor but I am still his mother!" were her words. We drove to Fort Meyers (me, John, and John Junior). We surprised my mother on her job at Red Lobster, she grabbed me for a hug and I was all smiles as she introduced me as "her boy" to her co-workers. While we went back outside and waited, she went into the kitchen and soon returned with some chicken, biscuits and chips.

We waited until her shift was over. She seemed overjoyed to see me. Muhammad and I were in the truck waiting and he convinced me or at least told me that he would convince her to let me stay with him, to help her "see the light." He wanted me with him at last for the entire summer because having kidnapped the child made it impossible for him to contact anyone to keep them, thus he needed my help to free up time for him to make some money. He explained that once this was done he would be moving to Canada and I can choose to come with him or stay with my mother. He also made it clear that regardless of my choice that we would remain in contact. He intended to do all of this by setting up a counterfeiting racket. What money he had left was being used to get hold of the machinery that was required. The last step being that he would return to Antigua in time to smuggle out a Jamaican friend who would be on bail in mid-August. They had worked together for three months prior to his arrest. John had $1,000.00 in samples that the guy had done for him in Antigua. He was using these to develop clientele, which he was doing at a rapid pace. John was now immersed in a circle of Jamaicans and Floridians who were in all sorts of what I now call "low reward, high risk" criminal activity. Such was the plan as it was explained to me.

To the matter at hand, we stayed at my mother's shared apartment for the night. John and I sat in her room and talked. My mom had a Haitian roommate in her mid-40's with whom she shared the house with. The entire place except for the bathroom and my mother's room was filthy. I mean there were cockroaches, stinky carpets, and three unwashed kids. It was just plain dirty. John pointed out that my mother could save her money faster and get stable if I stayed with him. She informed him that she was married and that things should be looking up soon. They talked all night as he tried to convince her, which he did, at least until it was time for us to leave the next morning. In the morning she took it up with John again. She kept looking at me to agree with the things she was saying, but I kept silent. She heard no protests from me. I looked at Muhammad who slightly nodded, indicating we were leaving. Her protests went on all the way until we dropped her off at Red Lobster. She got out and walked toward the restaurant, and then suddenly did a 180 degree turn. She grabbed the door of the truck and in her most stern voice said, "Lee you get out of this truck now!" She was livid and rather stunned when she realized that I wasn't the least bit moved by any of her words. I looked again to Muhammad who asked, "Son, you ready?" I responded, "Yes, sir!" John rolled up all the windows and reversed out of the parking lot. My mother stood there until she became a tiny dot on the horizon. I felt a little bit bad but I quickly corrected myself, she just would not listen. It seemed rational and best for all involved that I stay with John. In fact, right then and there I had made up my mind to stay with John. For real, I wasn't really happy to see my mother. Around her, I felt like I am being squished, stifled and robbed of living. John, well, I thought then he understood me, he listened, he appreciated me and took into account my perspective in almost every subject.

I grabbed a magazine and we left Fort Meyers, leaving my mother in the past. Two weeks passed as John amassed all the machinery that was required for the counterfeiting. He was now in the process of saving enough money to get a place for him. He intended to leave for a few days but was concerned about the children being that his previous departure was so stressful on them. He decided a new place, a laptop, and a few swimming classes would keep the girls occupied in his absence. He assured them that the trip would be a two-day at the most kind of trip, but he intended to be there in the morning. I was just happy to be in his presence, I admired his efficiency, order and ingenuity.

To my dismay, this was not meant to be, as my mother began calling multiple times daily, threatening to call the police and report that John had kidnapped her son. After listening to her hysteria, he didn't doubt her. He said he would try to work things out, smoothing things over a bit this time. "I will have to call and keep in close contact with her." John explained. I just sighed. "But sir, what is there to talk about?" John replied, "What shall I tell your mom?" I then thought silently to myself that he should tell her that, "she is being an unnecessary pain in the ass." What she held over me was not a coat of motherly love, but a burden of fear which was beginning to wear off. I just wanted to be free of her, I just did not know how. For sure, I had enough money, I would get myself some fake ID's from these Haitians and she would never see my face again. The most she would ever get from me were phone calls and money orders. I would do my best to learn this counterfeiting thing inside and out so that I could continue to Canada with John.

We drove again to Fort Myers, just the two of us this time. Once again he spent the night doing his best to let her see things his way. He tried every trick in the book, eventually returning to my mother's greatest weak point – money. He offered her money and free legal papers. John explained is opinion on my education saying, "it was useless for Lee to enter high school as there is nothing there him to grasp," and that he would simply have me get my GED instead. She frowned through his entire conversation. By the smug look on her face it was obvious that she was still unconvinced and unreachable. She had enough and stopped him mid-sentence saying; "Look, he is my child, what I eat he eats, if he cannot be satisfied with that - that greed will kill him." Looking at me she said, (with piercing eyes that indicated something sinister) "You are still my son, you belong to me, I am your mother. You met this man no more than six months ago and you've completely forgotten where you have come from." I was still young enough to shrivel up from hearing her harsh tongue. I sat motionless looking at Muhammad. She grabbed me and pushed me out the door to fetch my duffle bag.

She then told John to leave, which he did. That morning she bid me to follow her to Jacob's (a friend of hers) apartment. "Jacob?" I questioned. Once we entered his apartment and she began to spew to Jacob how Muhammad had control of me. She repeated how ungrateful I was and that I didn't love her. "You just met this man not even seven months ago and you listen to him instead of me. You are mad!"

Jacob explained that he had counseled her to keep me away from Muhammad because I was being introduced into a life of easy money. He went on to say something to the effect that, "Once you get addicted to it, you will be in deep shit and you don't want to get arrested in America, trust me." As far as I was concerned, when did this guy become a saint? When was he to be so concerned about my welfare? I went on to say to them, "I have always intended to move on to college." He gave me another lecture about the neighborhood where we resided. There were many ways to get into trouble around here. "Una, you better warn him because he's too stubborn, I am not going to sign my name to any paperwork only to have the police drag me out of bed." The following week Jacob took me to the clinic to get my shots and register for high school. I was soon thereafter introduced to Jeremiah Neal (Jay), my mom's new legal husband via a $3,000.00 business marriage. She explained to him that her son needed to get legal documents so he can go to school and to college. Jay faked earnestness and as soon as he grabbed another $400.00 or so, he disappeared. Jay would reappear whenever he wanted money, and would threaten to turn my mother over to the INS via a tip by making one telephone call. Jay was a dead beat, my mother attempted to pressure him by speaking to the

Jamaicans that introduced her to him in the first place. He would show up, do some sweet talking, and then disappear for a few weeks. I was also introduced to "Ras" (a Jamaican) who had been here for twenty years. He would throw a roll of money onto the passenger seat and tell my mother to come into the car. He would point to the roll saying, "You want that? You can have it, but not if you keep giving me the cold shoulder." He scared my mother, not that he was in any way trying to intimidate her, but because he had been a drug dealer for those 20 years. I noticed that when he drove up he would tell her to hold on while he took a few seconds to adjust his mirrors in order to give him an all-around view. He would then grab his 40mm semi-automatic from under the driver's seat and have it resting on the steering wheel. While talking and smiling, his eyes were always searching everyone that walked by as if he were searching for threats. Mom would reply after he left, "That man would kill something in a heartbeat Lee. You see the look in his eyes, his mouth is smiling but his eyes are searching all the windows and doors – he don't miss nothing." She told him to stop coming around. We got an apartment about four blocks up the street. It was a two bedroom apartment for $500.00 a month. It was the end of summer and I entered my senior year at Cypress Lake High School. I was placed in the standard classes: history, algebra II, English III and some ordinary science classes. In two weeks I went from algebra II to Trigonometry and from English III to English IV. By the end of November I was summoned to my guidance counselor's office. She reviewed all of my grades and explained that I needed to be preparing for college now. "How do I intend to pay for tuition, grants or scholarship?" I replied. She gave me some brochures and explained each of them to me. "Well Mr. Malvo, you take this 83% in Trigonometry to an 'A' and keep getting a straight 4.0 with the addition of a 950 plus score on your SAT and you may qualify for these two. All we need from you is to provide the previous two years of grades from other schools." She had looked at me funny regarding my years in Antigua. She went on saying, "I have been trying to get in contact with your schools to no avail. But most important are the essays. That will set you apart from your counterparts. If your writing is exceptional, then that is what will earn you the $5,000.00."

I completed a 3,000 word essay on Martin Luther King and I asked my English teacher to review it. She made a few corrections and told me it was "good stuff." I typed it at the library and submitted it to my counselor. The next step was the SAT exam. I needed a social security number and the entry forms for Embry Riddle and Florida A&M. I took these forms home to discuss them with my parents.

In the first week of December my mother and I attended a P.T.A. meeting which was for seniors. After the meeting my mother spoke with all my teachers. She spoke to my teachers and got excellent reports and compliments on my manners and work ethic. For once, she could not run her mouthpiece at me. It was explained to my mother, by the counselor, the importance of my applying early and what scores I needed to achieve on the SAT. I took a few prep tests at the library using the SAT preparation books and scored a meager 920. I realized that if I spent three to four weeks studying and touched up on my vocabulary, I could increase my scores by about 100 points.

Mom tried all sort of gimmicks. She went to Jacob who obtained two legal Haitian birth certificates. I pointed out to my mother a major glitch by saying, "Neither of us speaks French!" "How do we justify being Haitian without being able to at least speak their native language?"

By this time we were practically begging Jay for help, but all he wanted to talk about was money, another dead end. Without my mother's permission, I kept in close contact with Muhammad. She found out by spotting a Washington state number on the caller I.D. and warned me to stop speaking to "that man."

I continued to speak to him every Friday at 4:00pm. I tried softening up my mother when all other avenues turned up as a dead end. I told her that John could adopt me and I could be legal rather immediately. I am still 16 years old and we could get a birth certificate saying I was 15 and I would be legal almost instantly. After hearing this John called and told her that he would do anything he could to help me. Bombarded from both ends, it sounded good to her until she hung up the phone. I kept up the pressure as he had told me to do and got her to purchase a ticket. I then went to Kinko's and made copies. I gave her a copy and kept the original. The night before I was supposed to leave she went bezerk again. "No! No! He already wanted to take you from me; if he adopts you...I won't let it happen. You and John think I am stupid. I won't have any say so in your life." She went on for hours, threatening to give me a long deserved ass-whooping if I disobeyed her. I sat there impassively, waiting for her tirade to finish so I could pack my duffle bag and leave. Muhammad had told me they had taken the children number one, and number two, that he would help me get into college. Leaving with him seemed much more logical to me than staying with my fist-shaking mother.

She had tried in utter futility for the previous three months to cross the divide that the years apart had created. The problem was that I had become much more withdrawn, and only spoke when necessary. To make things worse, when I arrived we had started working Saturdays and Sundays at a small resort where we would clear rooms for $25.00 each. We did anywhere from 9 to 11 rooms a day. She had agreed that I would be allowed to keep half of what I earned. Upon receiving the checks, she told me that I would have to start chipping in. This meant I got nothing. One time she gave me $50.00 after I had pleaded for some new t-shirts because I only had six shirts for school.

She finally retired to bed in these words, "My way or the highway." Well, the highway it was for me. That morning I packed my few belongings; two sneakers, some t-shirts, a few pairs of pants, a tennis racket, a CD player and a few CD's. I snuck out of the house at 4:30am and I was on my way to Tallahassee by 5:15am. Once I reached Tallahassee I contacted Mr. Muhammad. "Sir, I ran way, I need some money for a new ticket!" He informed me to check Western Union in the next hour. He then asked, "Do you still have the I.D.'s?" I replied, "Yes!"

His instructions were very clear. "Get the tickets in the name of Lindburgh Williams in case you mother contacts the police. Stop off at the bus station for a few hours and place my bag in a locker, then leave the station. Change your shirt and other clothes and return about seven hours later. Then, at the next stop, do this again at all the major cities and come west!"

I followed his instructions and collected $1,300.00. I got my ticket as Lindburgh Williams and resumed my journey. I arrived in Bellingham, WA on December 5, 2001.

Chapter 13: Total Isolation

Upon returning to Washington Muhammad continues my training. His schedule for me became more demanding. First thing every morning was to go to the gym, then to the range or paint gunning, reading and watching videos. All my time, 24 hours a day, was spent under his tutelage and supervision. My Fridays would be spent debating with Earl, as I became more ardent and aggressive towards any view that opposed what Muhammad taught. I had never once stopped nor was I given a chance to be myself and critique his views. In any case, at that time, all I wanted was his acceptance so I swallowed all his distorted half-truths to get it.

One day, outside the Tacoma YMCA parking lot, I began questioning what he was doing. When he returned to the truck I had been sitting there by myself, reading, for about four hours. I thought about what he had taught me versus his own actions which were often contradicting. At this point I decided to confront him. I was sitting in the back of the truck when he climbed in and closed the door. Making sure I was out of arms reach I began my rant, "Why are you lying to me about Mary? All this black talk and you are fucking a white woman and don't deny it. She is more than just a close friend, don't feed me that bullshit. You said you are willing to do whatever it takes to get the children, how does she fit into the picture? She is just another devil. Didn't you say they are all the same; some are just better concealed than others? There is going to come a time, like the most Honorable Elijah Muhammad said, 'You will have to choose!' Right now you are choosing a cracker over your own children and if that time comes, make no mistake, I will kill you!"

I then put the .45 caliber hand gun where he could see it; my eyes were shaped into little slits of anger. John said nothing, not one word, he didn't even flinch. He started up the truck and I got back to my reading. He looked at me through the rear view mirror several times; his face remained the same unreadable mask. That day was the only time I had ever questioned him and he assured me that this would never happen again. He brushed it off that evening telling me that his relationship with Mary was over and that I was right. John said, "I see you are very zealous. We will see just how serious you really are."

Close to the end of November 2001 we returned to Bellingham, WA at night. John told me that while we were here a month ago, he was casing this place, not out of interest, but just his natural instinct to watch everything that goes on around him. He handed me the hand gun and told me that a lady will be coming to this parking garage. John said suddenly, "At 1:00pm she will have a money bag, simply shoot her and take it!" I looked at him incredulously, my mouth hanging open. I returned the hand gun to his possession. "Can't I just knock her out, with a piece of pipe or something?" He looked at me too closely for comfort, "Well, whatever it takes, just get the job done! When she comes the light will be off, you will only have a few minutes."

Her car was parked in front of the restaurant. "Sir, why are we doing this? Why are we doing this?" His eyes piercing into mine, "You are being prepared!" "For?" I asked. I realized that I had screwed up. I looked at the ground and he hissed, "Where is that zeal now? Are you going to kill me?" He laughed and then got serious again. "Are you willing to do whatever it takes? Are you? Are you?" "Yes, sir." I replied. "Then do it!" he yelled. John admonished me to "Improvise and use the crowd to your advantage. Can you pick the car door?" "Yes, sir" I did so and I got inside, then climbed into the back seat and hid. She came out, dropped the bag between the front seats, started the car, and then she paused. "Damn, I forgot the restaurant keys!" I sighed, thinking that now I don't have to hurt her. I grabbed the money bag and exited the vehicle. I took the trail on the bike I stole earlier that night; we met at the bus heading to Tacoma, WA. I gave him the bag. He went into the small restroom and searched the contents, retuning a few minutes later. John yelled, "There is a little over a thousand dollars and some insignificant checks, plus the coins are for the lottery." She apparently did not take out all the money for the restaurant. That day he went over the entire crime from the beginning to the end. He pointed out my errors and explained that in time, those would be corrected. To justify his madness, he had given me long lectures on how to detach myself. "You cannot be a black man without a stomach for violence." We then went to visit the projects of Tacoma, he pointed at the containment, not the elimination of crime and "parasitism" (as he called it). "Do you see those guys on the strip? Good. Now do you see the patrol car? I bet he knows the identity of every last one of them if he has been doing this beat for a while. But it is not a white problem, niggers are killing themselves. Its extension reaches the prison yards which are an economy, and as you see it now, a very profitable one. You see how many of them are your age Lee? Police protect the interests of the rich. They keep them going by controlling the streets. They are the circulatory system, they keep things flowing. So permanently you will have about 1.5 million of us incarcerated for life." He continued, "You see these young men, they probably all have time over their head. This is how they get you. While you are young and slinging, they bust you a few times, and slap you on the hand. They give you 20 years' suspended sentence without prejudice. Then after a few times they dish out what is left of the twenty years, plus the new arrest sentence. Basically 35-40 years of your life are gone! Because of the Darwinist process, there is only so much money to go around in this overcrowded environment. How many of us die today? Who gives a fuck?" The speech went on, "Now can't they work at McDonald's, nah! That is not really the image of manhood that society provides us (a booming, low-rider passes by us) that is the black man of this generation. I am a thug. That is the voice of manhood, or at least what we as a people are convinced it is. Welcome to the world of the hip-hop generation. Being it is easy, going along with the flow, the question is not to be or not to be, rather it is to think or not to think, to act or not to act. A child will be given to a foster home because his mom is on crack, a few dope heads will kick the bucket trying to seek out a worldly escape, who addresses our complaints? Who?" I would be caught in the convincing parts of his arguments. In fact, I was so blind with anger that his tone aroused feelings in me. I could only remain silent. How can I reject what he was saying here, as it is for me to feel, taste, touch and see?

We got back and worked out. When I finished my run I trotted into the house. Inside, they were making some strawberry flavored soy protein shakes. John patted me on the back, "Seven minute mile, not bad Lee, I guess that blows the idea out of the water that I couldn't actually catch you in Antigua!" He smiled and said, "You will get better, trust me."

I hear, "Leave that PlayStation alone and c'mon!" Now I was to be introduced to my regular weekend routine of stealing and going to the rifle range. John told me that the car we were sitting in, which is one I had never seen before, was his. It was a 1999 Infinity I30. His story was that he had given the car to a girlfriend before he came to the Caribbean. On our way to our first store he told me about how successful his many business ventures were and how Mildred (his ex-wife) and her friends destroyed all of that. Then he corrected himself saying, "It is my responsibility to keep my family together." We drove through two suburbs and he pointed to two houses and said those were both once his. While riding around we went into a K-Mart, Sears and a Wal-Mart. John stole small but expensive parts or tools and explained, "You see, because these are smaller I can easily walk out with 3 or 4 each for $90. Their size not only reduces the chance of getting caught, but so does this (As he removed a small circular magnetic strip and showed it to me on his finger tip).

We started with $530.00 and in about 5.5 hours of driving and visiting about a dozen stores we had over $2,000.00. "The trick is this," he explained, "Each store carries specific brands, many with identifiers which indicated that the product was from another store, another Wal-Mart chain, etc." If we lifted five $90.00 items at Home Depot, we would go to another Home Depot and return those first five stolen articles and receive a $450.00 "donation" as John would call it. Then he would come in after me with the receipt and five other items and steal five more of another item. Pay for another "duplicate" item with the money he got for returning the original ones. John explained, "When I was about seven years old I got caught stealing some lemon cookies. It was a dime for a small handful of them and I wanted to save my dime. I slipped up and got caught. First, I got an ass-whooping at the store, and then I received another when I got home, and that was from grandma. After that, I received a third beating from my grandfather. He whipped me real good, then sat me down and said, "I am not beating you because you stole, the fact is that I am beating you because you were dumb enough to get caught. Now, I am not encouraging you to go out and steal, but what I am saying is to use your head. If you are going to steal, think about it and the consequences. If you still decide that you can deal with the consequences, figure out the best way to do it and not get caught. You really like those lemon cookies? Answer me boy!" "Yes, sir!" John replied. (John was imitating his grandfather and his younger self) "Well, here is the entire bag of lemon cookies. Mind you, if you do not eat every last one of them, I am going to whoop your ass!" Muhammad laughed to himself at this memory then spoke to me in his monotone voice, "You see son, years later I grasped what he said to me. I didn't get my ass all tore up because I had stolen; it was actually because I was stupid enough to get caught."

When we arrived at Mary's place she was not at home. He grabbed some fish, bread crumbs, and seasoning along with rice and veggies and cooked us a meal. I spent the evening reading to Mary's granddaughter. I barely spoke to Alice, her second daughter, and

Shauntel her oldest daughter whose daughter I hit it off with really well. After putting her to sleep I went into the living room and played video games, wrapped myself up in a blanket and went to sleep. I woke up later and went on to beat the entire video game in 6 hours. As the next morning broke and before most of the others had awoken, I made Shauntel's daughter some vanilla flavored oatmeal, took out the trash, and washed and put away the previous night's dishes. I grabbed a book as the house came to life. Although the family was accepting I remained cautious and helpful, creating my own distance. Alice went to work around 9:00am and John and Mary lounged in private until around 11:00am that morning. Muhammad took a quick shower and made a phone call, then told me to get ready. I dressed in my jeans and sneakers and followed him to the garage. On our trek to three supermarkets, we filed in and out with bags of steaks and occasionally a few bottles of liquor. We arrived at Earl's place and handed him the binoculars and the bags of meat. Earl and I first got along quite well. He said to Muhammad, "Hey John, so you are taking him to the range, huh?" Then back to me, "Lee, you are going to love this, ever been shooting before?" "No." I replied. Earl remarked, "I will give you a thorough introduction." We placed all of the guns on the seat in the back of the truck and I climbed in next to them. I sat behind Earl and John on the way to Tacoma Sportsmanship Range. I contemplated what Muhammad told me while we were shoplifting meats for Earl. I soon was bestowed with another lesson. John states, "When you go bow hunting for a deer, you stalk, get up close and hit it, then you've got to track it. When you get close you never corner it because a hurt and scared animal with nothing to lose is a very dangerous one.

Therefore you give it a way out, but the way out you offer it needs to be your way. And that is the case with any animal, but it also applies to men. Like the deer, once you find its weakness, let him run away after being hit once. Meaning, after he has accepted a hit, allow him to bleed out until there's no more fight left."

Thinking back, it is weird how naïve I was to think I too was not part of a means to an end. John went on, "Earl will be a good lesson for you. It will be a test, and you have to learn to control your temper and detach yourself from your fiery emotions. They are just words, the meaning you give them leads to your reaction." Upon arriving to the range, John grabs his Remington 200 (.308 caliber), spotting scope, and targets. He goes directly to the long-range shooting area. Earl gives me a brief tour of the facility showing me first the archery area, then the hand gun range and finally the rifle range. Earl began instructing me about weapons, safety, and shooting. He gives me a .357 python. "Ok, now what do you do?" I point one hand at the target. He replies, "Wrong! The first thing you do is check your weapon. Is it loaded?" He instructed me how to check the chamber and never to point the barrel at a person when handling a weapon. He held up a .357 round and said, "This bullet will not say sorry, understand?" "Understood," I replied. Earl then provided me with the empty .357 handgun. "Now I will show you three stances. First, open your legs, shoulder width apart, square your shoulders, keep your hands fully extended and use your left hand to pull backwards. Ensure that you don't pull too much to the left or the right, this is to keep a steady aim." He then looked over, pushed my hand in plus, pushed down on my shoulders and told me to bend my knees a little more. We did this repeatedly, over and over again. Next, Earl explained that, "If you are in a house and you are after an assailant, you don't want to extend your hand fully when entering doorways." He then showed me how to make a perfect "box" with my arms, keeping the weapon closer to my body. He further explained that this stance is used in close quarters. He then explained the best thing, if possible was to find a rest. "If you can find a solid surface to rest your arm on, use it as a rest." This was explained that a rest would provide much greater accuracy and less trembling.

The next thing was the trigger. "Squeeze, do not pull a trigger. You need to practice doing that." Then he explained trajectory to me. Finally I got to shoot for the very first time in my life. I shot the .44 magnum, .45 caliber hand gun and a 9mm. I was terrible at it. Earl laughed, "Do you know why you are missing, well at least not hitting where you are aiming? One of the worst errors commonly seen is closing one eye. Unlike a scope, this is just normal sight. Ok, now put the weapon down." He went on, "Aim with your index finger at the head of the target. Look with your left eye and now your right. Did your finger seem to move? Now try looking down the center of your index finger with both eyes open while looking at the same target. Do you see that white dot, center it!" We went two shots to the chest and two shots to the head on the target. We repeated this pattern over and over again. We practiced until dusk. John returned and packed his long range rifles away. I strolled over to the rifle range where many younger kids were accompanied by their parents. There was this young girl there, no older than eleven or twelve I would say. She had a bull barrel .22 rifle and she was shooting with efficiency and with serene calmness.

This was admirable for I was still jumping from every bang as I shot each weapon. I went bezerk when I heard the .50 caliber go off. It was as loud as a tank cannon blast. I had been told that rifles have a kick that can be lessened with a muzzle break. I said to Earl, "That thing must have a real punch when you shoot it, right?" He replied, "Actually, no. It feels pretty much like an M-16 really." John asked Earl how I did for my first day. Earl remarked to John something to the effect that I had learned quickly, but I needed to practice squeezing, not yanking the trigger. He showed him my targets, from my first to my twentieth. "That's very good Lee!" John said. Earl remarked that at 25 feet or less I did okay, but any further I needed lots of work. John replied, "Next time, let him use the lithium sights on the 9mm and .45." Earl joked to John, "You should have seen his eyes when he shot the .45 magnum." Imitating my voice, Earl said, "Who would want to shoot this thing, it is too long, too heavy and way too loud!"

The following week I registered at Bellingham High School and started classes. I was taking AP Biology, Pre-Calculus, Government, History and college writing courses. With the exception of Pre-Calculus, I did exceptionally well. Missing half the semester in Pre-Calculus was disastrous for me, earning just a 73%. I was working very hard, but I knew by next semester with practice via CD-ROM math lessons from the local library, I would be back on track, well at least I could struggle to earn a B or B+. We went to the YMCA every day and discussed Black-American history, revolution, Elijah Muhammad and I got more lectures on why the white man was the devil. We went from 300 B.C. to current times. It was my crash course in the "war of the races." John would state,

"We live among the greatest murderer on the planet. It is manifested destiny; the calculated extermination of entire races of people. They are all the same.

I listened to Minister Farrakhan while I slept, but mostly I listened to Malcolm X's earlier speeches. He explained that African brothers cannot understand why black Americans cannot succeed. Malcolm X explained a basic fact. "Let us say that employment grows 2.5% yearly, now if the unemployed, welfare-looking black masses were to compete with the middle class white Americans on an even playing field, many of them would be out of a job, or rather displaced, which would be unacceptable." Malcolm X went on to say in one of his videotaped lectures, "We look in the mirror every day and we see a reflection of our black faces as we look at the world. Black is identified with everything self-negating, destructive, and yet we are blamed for all of America's ills. Blaming the victim!" Lectures like this along with reading, tapes and lots of running, shooting, and paint-gunning were now my weekly routine. John and I spent many hours together. My only respite was school. It was not that I did not appreciate all the attention John was providing, I craved it, I soaked it up, I absorbed his moves, his expressions and his personality and worldly outlook. What I feared the most was disappointing him. "We have fallen because of our disunity, selfishness and we must become one son, of one mind! A good leader must first be a good follower, a good instructor and a good listener."

I made audio tapes every night according to John's instructions. I read what the Muslims wanted. I read about Booker

T. Washington, W.E.B. Dubois and Malcolm X. What often put me to sleep was listening to Bob Marley and Buju Banton.

One evening we were at the YMCA shooting hoops and playing like father and son. Despite my ultra-competitive nature I could never win. So when he drove to the basket I would grab him by the waist. He just laughed and scored anyway. Now I called every foul and he would always reply, "You are such a whiner." "Watch this." I replied. He begins to complain about my unfair tactics, but to me it was just fun and games. He always won no matter how much effort I exerted. He goes up to shoot and I slap at the ball, but catch him in the face. I apologized and we continued playing. I grabbed him on the next drive to the hole and he swings his elbows to my jaw, grabbed my wrist between the joint and I am now on my knees in pain. Then he throws me about 10 feet across the floor. I am in a pile, holding my wrist when he looked at me with a hollow stare. I have never seen such anger aimed at me before from him. I immediately began to question, "What did I do to make him so angry?" He stared at me again, and then walked away. I blamed myself for the incident. I ran behind him, wanting him to explain why he got so violent with me, but he never even brought it up.

He never spoke about killing or shooting anyone during this time. He just said, "Every young black man should learn how to defend himself, shoot, and impart the practical lessons on how to succeed. Most importantly, he should learn who he is, that he is God! Not THE God but a God and he must never forget the wailing of his forefathers, bloodshed...begets bloodshed." He bristled further, "I don't know what we will have to do, but no man sitting on a bench in a black robe will tell me that I cannot see my children."

I wasn't calling my mother as often anymore. To be honest, we would probably have had another lengthy conversation. Whenever I called, I just handed the phone to Muhammad to end it. We traveled on weekends across the border to Vancouver. There he met with a few Indians. About what these meetings were and what was being said, I have no idea. Somewhere around December 23, 2001, my mother appears. John and I were returning from the gym talking about the salmon run and Darwin's theory of "survival of the fittest." As soon as we reached the steps of the Lighthouse Mission a man heads towards me from across the street and two men exit the Mission and blocked the entrance. John stands between me and these three men when one of the men pulls out a badge and points to me and says, "Lee Malvo, you are under arrest!" "Under arrest, under arrest for what?" I yelled back. There is a lady at the police station who claims to be your mother. I look at Muhammad and he just nods. They take me away. When I arrived at the station I am placed in a holding area, a small room separate from the others since I was a juvenile. My mother is brought into the room. "Is this woman your mother?" asks a detective. "Yes, sir." I replied. They allowed us to meet in private. I hugged her but gave her a look that said, "I am glad to see you, but what the hell are you doing here?" She had been accompanied by Reverend Al Archer. She had legal identification for herself, but it was in another name. Therefore, she could not prove conclusively that I was her son and thereby my legal guardian. In order to do this, she would jeopardize everything because she would have to use our Jamaican passports to prove she truly was my mother. She explained to the police that her identification is with her stuff and that it will arrive tomorrow. That explanation is immediately received by the police as suspect. "What the hell was she thinking?" I thought to myself. I was then placed with some child protection agency of sorts. Two days later I was at the police station once again. My mother hands them not only the Jamaican passports, but my birth certificate as well. The investigating officer lets us go, but makes a photocopy of our identification. Following our departure Reverend Archer takes us both out to dinner. They do most of the talking while I played with my food and listened. He later got us a motel room. My mother asked him if she can keep some of her stuff at the Lighthouse Mission's storage building. He replied, "You may do so as long as you want. However, you must be careful to stay away from John!" In the motel my mother and I hardly spoke. She chides me about running away and how this man (Muhammad) had complete control over me.

The next morning I went to school and John pops in mid-day and meets with my principal. We head to the YMCA once school is out and meet my mother back at the hotel in the evening. I told her to come with us to get a bite to eat. The three of us sat and had a meal together; however, she was a bit fidgety the entire time. Muhammad tries to no avail to convince her to drop the whole thing that I am "better off with him." "Who do you think you are?" she begins to raise her voice. John looks from side to side as the stares begin. She said, "Lee, c'mon, let's go!" She walks off and then realizes that I am still seated, looking to Muhammad for instructions. She turned around and in a pleading and desperate voice says,

"Lee!" Muhammad stands up, and then I stand up and we walk past my mother. She stands there, frozen. "How could you?" as her voice broke into a cry. She follows us onto the sidewalk. I cross the street with Muhammad and don't look back. In the storefront glass I see her reflection as she is leaning against a stop sign, sobbing.

I try to stress the point that the police are already suspicious. I said to John, "Let's leave tonight, it will only be a matter of hours, not days before they detain both of us and deport us." He replied, "When were you released?" "Yesterday, sir." "Ok, then we will leave tomorrow afternoon." As I entered the Lighthouse Mission, Jerry hands me a message. He looks at me rather gloomily. "A lady was here just a few minutes ago, it was your mother. She told me to give you this." He hands me some kind of letter or note and I stare deeply at it. I passed it to Muhammad who just threw it into the trash.

I was getting ready for school the next morning when Muhammad informs me that a friend put him into some serious money. It is money that we can make over the holidays, but he will need my help. I am still a bit down contemplating about how I handled my mother. John says, "It's about the children." Now he had my full attention. He doesn't tell me what his plan was as he never did. Information was always on a need to know basis. As John always said, "You never tell people more than is necessary, some things you will just have to trust me, understand?" I smiled, "Good, Good!" We head to the YMCA to get a few things from our locker. As we are packing up our stuff an INS officer walks into the locker room along with the director of the YMCA and says, "Are you Lee Malvo?" "Yes, sir" I replied. The officer takes out his cuffs and begins to put them around me. I give Muhammad an angry look. "I told you so!"

Chapter 14: Running Away for the Second Time

On December 27, 2001 my mom and I were both at the INS' adult detention center in Seattle, WA for two days. We were in the same cell. In passing, to see us both lying in separate bunks one would have assumed we were perfect strangers. I was brooding to myself over her stupidity. She would whine, "It's for your own good even if we get deported, can't you see it's for your own good?" For the two days I didn't even acknowledge her presence. They separated us and I was transported to the Spokane Juvenile Detention Center, while mom stayed in Seattle. I was placed in a cell and ate breakfast in the morning. I mingled with the other delinquents. Monday I was taken to the nurse for a check-up, I asked why she wasn't here all weekend, she explained that she was a Seventh Day Adventist. I explained to her that I grew up in the same religion and told her a little about myself, about Jamaica and the churches on the islands. I explained that I was a lacto vegetarian; she brought soy milk for my meals and assured me that I would receive a proper diet. It was the Christmas holidays so we were allowed to watch a few videos and if we behaved we received a Christmas bag each day with candy bars and sweets.

As within any social situation there were small groups of people; the cool, the not so cool, etc. I decide to sit with the girls; I played some cards and gave away my Christmas bag. Every morning we did calisthenics in the gym. A week went by without any problems. I was soon advanced to the second level. T-shirts with separate colors - orange, sky blue, green, and navy blue was used to separate everyone and let staff know instantly which level you belonged. As you go up the ladder your privileges increased, given more time outside of your cell during recreation time. We would return to our cells exactly in that order, first orange, then the sky blues, then greens, etc. Navy blues were allowed to have auxiliary jobs cleaning showers or helping clean up and prepare food in the kitchen. They were also allowed radio and made their own snack bags. My first incident was getting caught exchanging foods, or to be more specific, I was giving away my sweets and candy bars for salads. I was disciplined and simply stayed in my cell and ate my meals. Soon my school was contacted as the new semester had begun. The principal at the facility explained that I was at a juvenile detention center, etc., etc. I became much of a teacher's pet because of my work ethic. I enjoyed learning and I was attentive. Soon, I was given the task of helping others with their work in all my classes. I was also put in charge of calisthenics in the mornings.

By the time my mother had contacted an organization that defended alleged immigrants, we had spoken just twice. I was visited by a lawyer; my mother and I had discussed and agreed on a story that because she was married she couldn't be thrown out of the United States. Our story took some stretching of the truth so we said that she was severely abused and I wrote my statement which by no accident was the exact same as hers. Soon thereafter I was allowed to purchase a pre-paid phone card and contact my family overseas. I called Mr. Muhammad who told me that I would be out in a few weeks and I kept him up to date with the progress of my case and life in "juvie." With the help of a social worker and a very talented attorney we were released on bond and a date was set for our court appearance. I was flown to SeaTac and reunited with my mother in

Seattle. From there we returned to Bellingham, WA. On the way there I contemplated my staying in Bellingham. Maybe the story my mom had hatched would work but I had my doubts. Additionally I could not face my peers in school as my entire assimilation was now known as a farce.

We stayed in an abused women's protection center, which was really just a large house with seven or eight bedrooms in it. We were given a code to the security system which we had to use at the door. The house was located in an ordinary community just outside the city limits.

The second day of our arrival mom contacted Reverend Archer and asked if he could provide her with transportation as she tried to cash a check. We met with him at the local transit terminal and he drove us around all day, but at the end of the day we still had the check. Mom needed to cash the check so she could repay the organization which put up the $2,000.00 in bail. I told her of a few check cashing places around the mall. The next day we were able to get the check cashed. Later that evening mom was in the kitchen preparing dinner so I took $30.00 from her purse and headed directly to the Greyhound station. I had timed it so I could catch the 3:15pm bus to Tacoma, WA. Once I was in Tacoma I contacted Muhammad immediately. After two calls I found him at Mary's. I had assimilated his entire personality. My only goal from the first day in detention was to run away.

Chapter 15: The Devil You Don't Know!

Once released from custody I went back to Bellingham, WA. John was accompanied by Mr. Holland, (a.k.a. Don) a friend. They were waiting for me upon my arrival. John and I hugged and Don was introduced to me with a handshake. John asked if I was hungry to which I replied, "No, sir!" Our next stop was the Lighthouse Mission Ministries. John told Mr. Holland to give him a few minutes. We stopped at the front desk. Muhammad introduced me to Jerry, a gregarious old chap that was on shift. "This is my son, Lee. I need the forms; he will be staying here and is 18 years old." At that moment Reverend Archer exited his office. When he saw John he walked right over. John introduced me to Al (Al Archer). Al's tone was brisk yet friendly. It took about fifteen minutes and we were cruising with Mr. Holland to work. They were working on a house, among other things. The day was pretty much uneventful, they did their carpentry and plumbing while I handed them tools that were needed. I just listened to their conversations.

Mr. Holland dropped us off at the Mission midafternoon and we walked to the organic food store. We got some smoked salmon and avocado sandwiches. John said, "We will eat here on most days." The Lighthouse Mission was a homeless shelter with half its occupants on some psychological medication and the rest were just hopeless. The members of the Mission have all been in and out of prison and are basically lifetime losers. It was best that we kept to ourselves and conversations to a minimum. Bible study was the more socially interactive portion of the day, which was at 6:00am and 7:00pm.

"We will be busy all day during the week and we will be gone on weekends, understand!" "Yes, sir!" I replied. "Good! Now explain to me everything I just told you." I did, as he requested and he nodded. When I was finished he nodded in approval. We spoke about Florida and my mother. "Well, we need to call her. You will do that tonight!" He looked at my face which was clouded with worry, then he laughed, "Don't worry Lee; I will smooth things over with her." We've got some dates and some green tea. John said, "Tomorrow we will go out with Don and get you signed up at the YMCA, then hit the bus to Tacoma." We returned to the Mission, sat in the front row and went through the motions. I went upstairs to the laundry room and was given some linens and assigned to a bunk.

We arose early that Friday morning. We called my mother, John did all the talking. He was on the roster to prepare breakfast. We headed into the large basement which served as the chow hall complete with a kitchen. The floor doubled as a sleeping space at night. I offered my services and was relegated to setting the tables, after which I returned beside Muhammad who was in gloves and to my surprise preparing the bacon. He kept at the task silently as if thinking carefully to answer my questions. When he was finished, he called me to the counter where they had begun serving the morning meal. "Hey Boys, we got some more Canadian bacon left for seconds!" A few whistles and a booming "Yeah!!" came from the tables and soon there was a line. After all the bacon was gone he said, "As we travel you will see that in a free society, amid all your free privileges, you could do everything properly and you will still be viewed as a nigger. It is a pleasure to watch the devils eat themselves to death, rather a slow suicide."

He saw the rather confused look on my face, "Don't worry you will understand." He didn't eat (he only ate one meal a day). Under his instruction while I was in Florida I practiced eating only twice daily. He informed me that in time I would graduate to the next step. That morning I began my day with a cocktail of vitamins and eating between 4:00pm and 6:00pm. We went upstairs after we helped clean the tables and wash the dishes. We strolled up to the front and listened to the reverend speak about Jesus. When they all clapped their hands and closed their eyes to pray, John and I locked eyes and just shook our heads. While we helped fold and stack the chairs he said, "Lee, don't you want to go to the land of milk and honey?" I replied, "Yeah, sure. The honey is in my back pack along with date and yogurt covered raisin, the milk is in the store a few quick steps and ah! Heaven!" I smiled. He winked, "But the contract with the blue-eyed God (Pointing at the mosaic of Christ on the chapel wall) is as follows: suffer, eat, die poor, love and forgive those who kill you and all good things will come to you after life's beautiful end. A rich man can never make it to heaven. Heaven is for the meek, humble, pure in heart and dead in the head!"

While signing out we encountered Reverend Archer. John answered all his questions. I took my lead and excused myself. I stood outside thinking to myself, "man this place is cold." I felt a hand squeeze my shoulder, "Here!" as John handed me a jacket. "Don't worry Lee, you'll get used to it."

"Good morning John!" Don said. "And young chap how are you doing this morning?" I smiled and replied, "Just fine, sir." We hopped into Don's car. Don said, "On the way up John and I will be stopping at the supermarket for a pack or two of mountain dew, do you need anything Lee?" "A large bottle of water will be fine sir!" I replied. Don and John cracked jokes as we drove to the apartments just outside the city limits. During the day I handed them tools and listened to their conversations. John always returned to getting full custody of his children, or he'd satisfy Don's curiosity about me, "Well, will be registering him in school next week and he will be going to flight school as soon as I get some things straightened out." When I wasn't being handy I raided the dozen or so apple trees, slicing up apples and gulping them down with raisins and two protein bars as soon as my watch beeped 3:30pm.

We went to the YMCA and played basketball, then grabbed a bite at the local "food-to-go" and took the local transit to the greyhound station John surprised me by giving me a few CD's (Tupac Shakur, Tracy Chapman, and a speech by minister Louis Farrakhan). I slept through the ride. I woke up to hear "Come on son!" We walked into the small Tacoma terminal where he greeted and embraced Mary, who had heard enough about me and greeted me like family. I placed the small bag I had into the trunk of her car. John ushered Mary to the passenger side, ensured that she was safely seated and we drove to her place. That night I ate pizza with her family and slept in her son's room, as apparently he was at a friend's place for a sleepover. After playing basketball and PlayStation through most of the night I fell asleep.

Saturday morning John and I went for a run. Mary rode her bike. As usual, John gave me a head start, actually about a 6 minute head start. I took off like a rocket. After about a mile and a half I felt a tap on my shoulder, then saw a large smile and then his outline began getting smaller and smaller as he headed back to our starting point. I wanted to be just like him, to see the big picture, to make some positive changes. My idealism fogged whatever vision I had left.

What thoughts occupied my mind was what I was told to consider. I needed to address my remorse and pity. John would say, "You must remove and set aside your moral compunctions, you must become objective, what is, is, yes! But it is not absolute, it is because you and I allow it to be, we allow it to exist. What we need is the resources and the time to de-program a generation. We need a few trained men and women who have grown beyond the far reaching tentacles of Eurocentricism, so that they can be educated to function in the system while planning to destroy it."

John went on, "People will not change or a change will not come about until they, the people, first identify that there is a problem and they are willing to make the necessary internal and mental changes necessary to overcome the outside obstacles. You will have to fight daily to remove the Willie Lynch in you."

You see, I was somewhat of an idealist, enjoying cerebral discussions, dreaming of change. I had not yet grasped the fact that change is usually a very slow process. All I wanted was his attention. There is one discussion that is one of the more memorable because it highlights all of the hallmarks of what was being done to me before my eyes. John explained the French Revolution as, "One beginning with ideas but not allowing it to end there. You have to feed the ideas, propagate them, incite the people, move them, and lead the blind masses for their own good."

"Make your ideas their ideas, by clothing it in the proper context. You can make anything acceptable, it is about presentation, but most importantly, timing." He continued as if talking to himself, "You have to reach the agitated minds at the most opportune moment, a young naïve mind is like a small tree. One has to feed it, prune it and lead it to growth. It is easy to sell a lie, the truth on the other hand is fixed, a lie is flexible, always moving and continuous."

These were not discussions, rather one way lectures. He, the master, and I, his disciple. He drilled into my mind at every opportunity some hate-filled message. Whether we were in a café, on the bus, at the gym, eating out, it was everywhere - 24 hours a day. Anger makes a man blind and he intended to keep angry at the white man and keep the focus away from himself. Keep the lie going, never giving you time away from his influence long enough to test his assumptions. All his lectures were openly telling me what he was doing to me, but I couldn't see it. The thought that I was just a means to his insidious ends never crossed my mind. I wanted so badly to believe in something he became long ago - the object of my hopes, admiration and of my beliefs. Aptly put, one could easily say I idolized him. He became more convincing, more cajoling, and more rewarding. My reward was his attention. I know how silly that sounds, but the truth often hurts. John said, "Do you know the principle of need-frustration?" "No, sir!" I replied. "Ah, let me explain."

John would go on, "Let us begin then with a practical example. Let us consider the human development to be like that of a developing body, one with nutritional and psychological needs. In this case let us use Vitamin C or even calcium for the strength of the bones, that is calcium and for the prevention of scurvy - that is the Vitamin C. It is a necessity that the human diet provides the essential amount of each. Now, when this need is frustrated and by this I mean the demand for the aforementioned substances is not satisfied, the consequence is not immediate, but the body is an inter-dependent mechanism. If one link in the chain is missing or is malfunctioning, it affects the entire system. If for example the circulatory system is clogged or affects the amount of oxygen that reaches all organs, and the transportation of the much needed nutrients and also waste of one organ is unable to fulfill its functions, then that puts pressure on the others organs. In time, these or any other deficiency leads to not sudden death, but a slow, constant attack in the body's ability to satisfy the demands we place upon it."

"In the case of blacks, we have become apathetic; rather accepting what is, as all that we can and will be, the change in them from birth until death took time. The constant attrition leads to a premature end for when all these multiplied deficiencies begin to manifest the overall effect, it is far too late. The death we live son is not a sudden one, it is a leeching process. You become the living dead before you die."

On and on John would say, "So the same principle applies to us, if our goals are separation and our approach different, that leads to a growing dichotomy, there can be no schism, we are inter-dependent, and we must be of one mind. Unity is life, unity is order, and chaos is confusion and death."

"If the intent is to reprogram an individual, it is impossible to rewire their experiences; rather one should build on what they already have. One has to become a ghost, an unseen catalyst that causes change but remains intact. One has to facilitate the means and ways for that change to come into existence, knowing when to turn up the pressure and when to hold the reigns."

John provided an example of this when we were in Portland, Oregon. We were returning home from the YMCA and we stopped to sit on a park bench. Across the street was a Catholic church that serves as a soup kitchen for the poor. "Son, to reach the objective the correct ingredients must be mixing in the pot," he pointed across the street as he munched on a protein bar. "I see impatience; anger, a diffused aura of self-hate, a feeling of being nothing but an aggregate of all the necessary composites. Come on!" We crossed the street and join in the line. He begins again, "What the fuck is taking so long?" He turns to a man beside him saying, "It was the same shit as yesterday!" He touches another on the shoulder, "Every mother fucking day these crackers tell us to line up in the hot fucking sun, standing in the street like dogs." He goes on until a few men in the back start speaking up. John's speaking is actually slowing down the line. Some pushing starts, "Get the fuck out of my way!" an old man says. "If you make so much of a racket, the priest will turn us away!" "Fuck the priest!" Muhammad says to the old man. Muhammad taps me on the shoulder, "Keep them angry!" He winks to me and says to an old lady at the door, "Who the fuck are you looking at like that? I am black, but I ain't no dog!"

In about 15 minutes the hobos are storming through the door, cursing, demanding that the old white people speed it up, shouting and breaking chairs. He decides to leave it as it is. We returned to the YMCA, got our belongings and headed off to the greyhound station.

John continued, "And that is on a very small level, impoverished people everywhere are like a nice powder keg, waiting for a spark. They are already angry, just bring it to the surface and they will fight for nothing, just get them boiling, then direct their aggression."

During this time, in early February 2002, he borrowed an older model Ford F-150 from a Muslim brother of his. He comes up with an idea. Schuck's/Kreger's Auto Parts returns three receipts to their commercial customers. One is for bookkeeping; one is for taxes and whatever else a business needed. Knowing this, John checked his memory and recalled twelve telephone numbers of small mechanics' shops. The telephone numbers were used as the business identity at Schuck's.

Once again, he bought relatively small but expensive parts, with prices ranging from $90.00 to $135.00. In the western half of the state of Washington, John knew most of the managers because he used to own Express Car and Truck Mechanic, a service which provided a vehicle for the day. If your car broke down anywhere on the interstate, really anywhere at all, John would do the diagnostics on the spot, get the parts and fix it right there. If you were at work, he would take your car during your lunch hour; perform a tune up, fix the breaks, whatever was needed.

Armed with the extra receipt, we stole the needed parts. We spent three days just buying and stealing. From 9:00am to 1:00pm and from 2:00pm to 7:00pm we would go to the gun range.

For a month we did this scam of his and turned a pretty decent penny, over $5,000.00. When he went into return a part, I would return a part in another line. We did 8-12 stores daily. He had drawn maps with "X's" on the stores we had covered; we did the entire western half of Washington. The only money we spent was for gas and food. Even on the days when we went to the gun range, "Now son, take that look off your face. You look like you just committed murder." he laughed.

He would then resume his blank monotone voice, "You must be able to mask your intentions, so let me show you different poses. These men speak different languages but body language is universal. All these are aggressive postures; these are anxious postures, and most importantly, your eyes. Okay? Watch this, you see him? Yes, the target is now a man, can you see him? Clothe the target; give it a face, a personality. This man must be dominated, those are my orders. His family, his feelings, his pain is inconsequential and irrelevant, and pretty much none of my concern. I do not contemplate these things."

With these instructions, I focused all my energy on the task at hand. I am an instrument, unfortunately, an instrument of death - but a precise instrument nevertheless. I do the necessary reconnaissance, study the target, become not only acquainted but comfortable with the target's routine. I am now at ease in his surroundings. I am his shadow, that of death.

My opportunity comes and I have been patient. Yes, I have planned for every conceivable scenario, but the truth is, humans are not robots. You cannot stop the child from bursting out of the elevator or a man from being in the wrong place at the wrong time.

Mentally you must be aware of this, you cannot afford to freeze. As John would often say, "You must be like water, fluid; you bypass, overcome or go through the obstacle."

John turns, squares his posture and fires, removing the head of the little cardboard man, and then resumes his monotone voice, "You will learn to sit at the table with the enemy, talk with him, eat with him, eliminate him and not let any attachment stop you. What we feel is based on our morals, right and wrong, these are mutable concepts. Right and wrong do exist, right is that which satisfied and meets the demands of the current situation, this achieving your ends, wrong is to be mistaken, to miscalculate, and to fail."

John continues, "Think of what you saw yesterday, each of those lackeys slinging, peddling, society classifies you and them as one in the same. Here!" He then hands me the .45 caliber handgun. "Visualize what you saw, that target is your enemy, how do you feel? Let him taste your pain, feel it. Violence is necessary. It is for this that animals have claws. Men create and use weapons, the greatest of which is the mastery of his mind. The mind is your go-between with reality. It is your true eye to the world, be conscious of your thinking for what the mind says the body does!"

"Free your mind!" He smiled. "Now son, look at your handiwork, didn't even realize you discharged the weapon, eh?" He gives me a firm pat on my shoulder. "I dare say you did much better than I." He was cajoling, persuasive, encouraging and of course teaching by example while giving his instructions. The man had charisma.

"See what a little motivation can do, do you remember that place you were at, the place where your mind was blank, and your only thought was the task at hand. Visualize, place yourself in that zone. Leave your old self, the one that believed in the mystery God. Where was he when you were sick, without food, did he hear your cries? Did he? Did he?" "No, sir!" I replied.

"You are an instrument, whenever you conscience gets in the way, do this." (He hits his left pectoral muscle on his chest with his right fist really hard). Call your heart to rest, distill your thoughts, still your mind, concentrate, go over what has to be done, think of possible escape routes, don't think it, be it, you are what you think. Watch your eyes, observe what your eyes really see, get your heartbeat down, stop blinking so often, ask why am I perspiring?" He then pats me on the back, "The only one who can do it is you, I can give you the pie, but I can't force you to eat, free your mind!"

John would often say, "Lee, just think, you are meeting unpreparedness with preparation, you have won before the fight begins. It is not strength or even will, or even still, the man who is able to anticipate the next move and prepare for it with speed and precision is the one that wins. It is essentially the better thinker that wins!" The next night John drops me off, dressed in a dark hoodie and jeans, with shorts underneath. He says, "Now explain the plan to me."

"I am to knock on the door and ask for "Isa." If the person who answers is not her; I tell them I have a message for her. Then I pull out the .45 semi-automatic hand gun (my eyes are watering as a paper target is different from a living, breathing, animate human being) and I fire!"

His voice takes on an edge, "Where is your pledge?" I reach in my wallet and remove my half of a $50 bill. He continues; "And what is that on your half?" "Blood, sir." I replied. John asks, "Representing what?" "My word, sir!" He prodded me again, "And what word is that son?" "That I am willing to do whatever it takes to please you!" "And what does that really mean?" "That means without bounds or barriers, anything and everything, sir." John then went on with, "And a man is nothing without what son?" He said very slowly for effect. "His word, sir!"

John questions me further, seeing if I could repeat what he had drilled into me, "And what is right and wrong?" I replied, "The claims that the legislators use to enslave the legislated, rules by which they, the legislators themselves, are not bound. Morals are not immutable concepts but justification for actions that are necessary to satisfy the demands of the circumstances, sir!"

John went on with one of his countless political speeches, "Lee, you have to see the big picture. Stop getting trapped in all the details, the minute pixels. I share with you a tale from history."

"Wilson screwed up with World War I and the League of Nations was a failure. Now Roosevelt and Churchill first used propaganda to prepare the American minds, ideas my boy, ideas move mountains. But time had not erased the memories of lost sons, the people were still reluctant. America's involvement was detrimental to the West, who of course let the dog loose. But they were not afraid to use the chain. You see, as long as Hitler used up his lesser neighbors, there was no problem. The problem became a world problem once Hitler decided to exterminate them!"

John spoke, "Roosevelt knew of Japan's planned attack, but he calculated that America would rebound and the attack could serve as a "wake up call" that brought the war home to our hearts, and to our families. This was needed to overcome the impasses of the American reluctance. To this end, he sacrificed 8,000 men, because the truth was that the means justified the ends. To stay isolated while Germany conquered the West, to face a Germanized Europe, was inconceivable, rather disastrous. It was mere collateral damage that these men died."

He continued his rant with, "The devil must be respected because what he shows through his actions is that men conquer, take, build, create and control. When man played the same game during his explorations, all moral compunctions were set aside, discarded really, because they became obsolete and inapplicable. Right and wrong do not exist as morals and God is dead, now go!"

I walked out of the car. I tuned into his voice, all the lessons, all the preparations going through my mind. I thought to myself, "70 beats per minute, 69, 68, 67, 66, 65, be 'the calm'. The calm, cool, and collected survive. Free your mind to the task at hand, don't think about it, become it."

Knock! Knock! "This is mere karma, your harmony is resolute." Knock! Knock! "Men kill, men don't fight! Men initiate action, not passive reaction." The door opened. "Good evening…is Mrs. Nicholas in?" I asked. The young lady at the door seemed eager to talk for she gave me a long answer, telling me exactly the location of Mrs. Nicholas' whereabouts.

"I have a message for her." I reached into my paper bag, turning my body so she could not see my hand and a voice deep in me said, "Don't, Don't, Don't!" I thought, "Lee, you cannot face John unless you do this!" She inhaled, growing more impatient. (This all happens in a few seconds). I pointed the .45 caliber gun to her face, and in an instant I saw not her, but me, my old self that I hated, that scared, hurt self. That night, Lee Boyd Malvo died. I pulled the trigger. In an instant, she too was gone. (Such memories cannot be erased; they haunt me to this day).

I walked away as if I was a pedestrian headed for the bus stop on the corner. I reached the corner, walked down the alley and began to sprint downhill, crying silently, then the tears streaming as I hauled ass because now I am really scared. I think to myself, "Lee, calm your heart. How many beats? Get your breathing under control!" I hit the road in my shorts and a t-shirt. I go to a phone booth and pretend to make a call. John drives up and I throw him a football, "Father and son, eh?"

I sat silently, trying to hide my shaking hands from his gaze. "I watched you the whole time, you did perfect!" He smiled. I returned his smile. John said, "Don't worry, everything will be alright. Here!" He handed me my wallet saying, "This is your new name." I read to myself, "John Lee Muhammad," which had been printed on a New Jersey driver's license.

We went to Earl's and returned the weapon to its box. We had used a "dum-dum" round, no ballistics. "All your clothes are to be incinerated!" He turns on the news. Earl looks at me and smells that something is amiss, but what exactly he is not sure. I go to shower and remain under the water for three hours. Knock! Knock! I turn off the water and dress into my towel that is resting on the door. "You alright?" "Yeah." I responded. "Well get out of the shower Lee, this is their house!"

A few days later while in the Seattle bus terminal I told John, "Sir, I have a feeling my mother is here!" He raises his brow. I look three seats down and there she is, she spots me and runs, grabbing me by the arm. She cursed Muhammad and tells the driver to stop the bus immediately. Yelling loudly, "This is my son, he ran away to this wicked bastard!" (Pointing to Muhammad).

When the bus came to a stop, Muhammad got off and I followed him. My mother is still holding me by my coat. "Lee, I am your mother, don't turn away from me, he is using you." I am struggling to get out of my coat. I see Muhammad stop at the top of the stairs towards the exit, just looking at me. I turn slowly and look at my mother straight in the eyes. I am in the zone and slip out of the jacket and run to John. I hear in the distance, "This day you run from your mother to your death, you hear me Lee, to your death!"

Chapter 16: The Puppet Master

February 18, 2002 was my seventeenth birthday. John took me shopping and purchased a few items of clothing for me. We discussed my desire to return to school. He promised me that in early 2003 I would be enrolled in flight school, but for the remainder of 2002, he needed my help to get his children. We went bowling, I was a novice so I lost every round, be we had fun.

We also went to the cinema to see John Q. The emotion that surfaced within me reinforced my perception of Muhammad as the father who was willing to do whatever was necessary to be with his children. The next two weeks were spent in two ways. We were either at the rifle range and then the gym or we were collecting the money from a scam we ran on Schuck's/Kreger's automotive outlets, which netted close to $5,000.

In early March we headed south to Tucson, Arizona. In all prior trips we had used a vehicle, but because we had guns and rifles on us, Muhammad decided it was best to ride the Greyhound. This day long ride was prolonged into a three week ride. We first stopped off in Oregon, there in a large national park, Muhammad finished up what he needed to teach me about stalking. My test was to learn how to be completely still in adverse, cold, wet conditions, how to move undetected and to prove this by stalking hikers or campers. I would get but a few feet away from them undetected. We also tested two suppressors; we settled on one and destroyed the other. John's oldest sister resided in Tucson, Arizona. So a day before our arrival John had contacted her. She picked us up and dropped us off at a motel. She spent some time with us during the next two weeks whenever her schedule permitted.

The reconnaissance began by frequenting areas we thought the target would visit. Very quickly we spotted an elderly gentleman in a pharmacy that was in a strip mall close to where this man lived. John was gregarious and picked a conversation with this gentleman. The man was friendly and before I knew it, he was cracking a few self-deprecating jokes about his bad back and aching knees and his love of golf. He elaborated further that he spent most of his time on a nearby golf course. Through the information gleaned from this conversation, John decided that we needed to visit the park bordering the golf course to see if that venue presented the best opportunity for a shot. Under the pretext of exercising with his sister, we visited the park. I separate myself from John and his sister. I walked the trails and discovered that the desert offered little in the way of cover. The following evening John tells me to get dressed. He then hands me a bus ticket, and my back pack which contained: water, protein bars, dried cranberries, granola, a full day's supply of vitamins, desert camouflage fatigues, boots, a sleeping bag, some plastic bags, pencils and a drawing pad. John said, "I want a full description of the targets' routine. I need a detailed map of the park. I want you to highlight on the map the escape routes and the best places to take a shot. I need for you to clock the escape routes, understand?" "Yes, sir." I replied. He hands me the binoculars.

I arrived at the park around 5:30pm that evening. Once it got dark I changed into my fatigues and boots. I decided it was best to sleep off the ground. I slept uncomfortably on the somewhat flat surface of a boulder. I awoke at 3:30am. I washed my face and stretched. I ate a protein bar, granola and a handful of cranberries then I took my vitamins, thirty-six tablets in the morning and thirty-six tablets in the evening. I ate one meal a day. I had spent the last year (2001) eating two meals a day and gradually I progressed to one meal a day. I was following the dietary prescriptions as outlined in Elijah Muhammad's *How to Eat to Live*. These changes and others, which included the teachings of the Nation of Islam, began in Antigua. I spent the next five hours learning the trails. I walked along the edge of the golf course, just learning the terrain. I had a map to make and went about it gradually. I collected a dozen golf balls that were in the areas closest to the course. Around 9:30am I located the target, he was putting. I was flat on my stomach; I had concealed myself so that a passerby would be hard pressed to spot me. He putted until his friends arrived. I made sure to stay at least 50 feet away from the edge of the golf course as I shadowed the target up until 3:30pm or so. Curiously, the target stayed behind and collected balls with a hand held machine. He would meander off the course, out into the surrounding areas, looking for golf balls. The target repeated the same exact routine three days in a row. He was always the first to arrive, punctually at 9:30am and once he had completed his round of golf he meandered into the area surrounding the golf course, collecting golf balls. On the third day, I made a note of this - that the target could be lured. By the end of the third day I had drawn a detailed map. I also decided that it would be best to obtain a bicycle, as biking was quicker than jogging. I had jogged the five possible escape routes; each was for a different shooting position. It was possible to shoot from a long distance, but John

always stressed that he wanted to take the "path of least resistance."
The simpler, the better. The target could be lured into the woods,
twenty or more feet away from any onlookers, thus the crime would
not be detected for at least an hour or so. His body could be dragged
and concealed – a place/spot prepared for its storage.

At the end of the fourth evening I returned to the motel. I
knocked, using a code Muhammad had taught me. When the door
opened I paid my courtesies and headed immediately for the shower.
Once I had cleaned up we shared a pizza then I explained my maps
and shared my notes. I told him about luring the target. He could
then conceal the body if he wanted to do so. I also explained that I
needed some money to purchase paint and a lock cutter. I purchased
the aforementioned items that evening and stole a bicycle which I
then spray painted in a different color. Upon my return, John
informed me that I would be taking the shot. I felt unprepared for
this task and I spent the next hour or more in a futile effort to
persuade him that he should be the one to take the shot. John
listened intently to my protestations without interrupting me, his face
an unreadable mask. Once I had exhausted my reasons why I could
not, he asked me, "Are you finished?" Before I could respond, he
went on to say "Nothing in itself is right or wrong. The motive
alone behind the action dictates the outcome, the consequences. You
have stated many reasons, but what is left unstated is the real reason.
So, what are you afraid of?" I opened my mouth to answer, but
John's upraised palm silenced me. He chuckled, and then said, "Ah,
I see you still have not mastered Chapter 7 of *Don't Sweat the Small
Stuff, It's All Small Stuff: Don't Interrupt Others When They are
Speaking*. John said, "May I continue?" I nodded, assenting for him

to continue. John takes out a torn fifty dollar bill, his half. Seeing this, I too took out my half of the fifty dollar bill. Each half had a bloodied fingerprint symbolizing our blood pact. He silently looked at the bills and placed the halves before me as one bill. "Do you recall the pledge we made? We pledged to do whatever it takes. Do you understand – now – whatever it takes means?" John went on to explain, "Whatever it takes to get this family back together. It means no limits, no boundaries."

"Trust and patience son. I have been your age but you have never been mine. You don't know what you are yet capable of. Your fear has its root in your attachment to wrong thinking. You have been taught and believe in the hand-me-down, half-assed logic that you have inherited, unwittingly, unknowingly, from your fore parents."

John went on to say, "Right now, the question that is gnawing at your psyche. The question that went unasked is, how can I justify killing this man? How will his family be affected?" John removed the seven pictures of the man from a manila envelope and laid them out from the largest to the smallest before me, and then he continued. "The white man is either – the devil – or your friend. What you spent the last week doing was to reverse however minutely a process the Caucasians have used to successfully conquer – all native people the world over. You secretly invaded his life, you studied his movements, his character, you found the best opportunity to achieve the aim you seek and – you will exploit – prosecute – that advantage to such an end. The white man had no squeamishness when it came to trade, slavery or any other system of exploitation."

"There is no mystery. God, Heaven and Hell are in the state of your own consciousness. You experience the world as you think it; nothing is ever good or evil, only thinking makes it so. As an example, had you not planned to join the military? The people you would be killing overseas are justified only because society sanctions such murder. This is the same society that at its birth deemed slavery acceptable. So, if you were off in the war, would you have any qualms with pulling the trigger? Would any of your combatants have been an enemy who personally injured you? No! Life is ever a war, you cannot escape it – none of us can."

John continued with his speech, "Stop policing yourself. Relinquish your old way of thinking. You see, this is why – you must – do this! You need experience. Survival of the fittest is just that. Slavery was but a means to an economic end – it was not personal. Without any half-doubts they did what was necessary to secure a bright future for their progeny."

"Telling yourself what you can and cannot do or be makes it real – in your individual reality. The problem lies squarely within the confines of your own thinking. Who taught you these values? Are your ideals truly your own? Your so-called moral compunctions hold you hostage. We are an ass-backwards people. We believe without examining the source to see if it is grounded in reality, applicable to our circumstances and can be validated if tested. We simply have been content to absorb unwittingly the morays and ethical system that has its roots in the institution of physical and mental slavery - the Willie Lynch fear mongering. This world is as cold as it is beautiful, prayer without action is futile. No amount of wishful thinking will put food on your plate, no miracle will be rendered at your weeping behest; manna surely will not fall from the sky. You have been given a mode of existence – a mind – use it! But first, detangle it from your cob-webbed thinking. Free your mind!"

"We have bought into a love of misery. We have been taught and have sought value-meaning. Purpose is always outside ourselves in a culture, a way of life that at its inception did not have our interest in mind and categorized us as beasts of burden for the more civilized of humankind. We have always had to try to be whiter, brighter, more cultured – just to be considered."

"We cannot escape the grasp of our collective past, our collective memory. You are still a slave. You cannot be free without unshackling yourself. Do you now see my meaning? You cannot be half-happy, half-doubtful and successful in the endeavor of emancipating yourself from mental slavery."

Having said more than his peace, John left for his daily five-mile run. I got my tape recorder and made my tape with quotes from the reading John had assigned me and excerpts from Malcolm X's early speeches in the NOI (Nation of Islam). I went to sleep listening to this tape.

The following morning I departed around 3:30am on the bicycle. I rode the many miles to the park. Once I arrived, I changed into my fatigues and began to create my lure. I set the dozen or more golf balls so that they would lead the target thirty to forty feet away from the golf course. The spot I chose had a small knoll with roughly a twelve foot slope. I concealed myself and waited. The target came down the knoll. He immediately spotted the balls, he followed them zigzagging towards the last ball. Once he reached the final ball I fired. I aimed for the heart as I wasn't confident enough to take a head shot.

I changed clothes, broke down the .308 and put it in its case that then went into my back pack. I trotted the distance to the target and pulled him further under the underbrush. I returned to my previous position, grabbed my back pack, trotted to the bike rack and rode the remaining distance to the entry of the park where I parked the bicycle on a rack – the bike had served its purpose. I then walked to the bus stop. I was surprised to find John at the bus stop waiting for me. He handed me a soft drink and returned to the book he was reading. The bus came and went twice; we didn't leave until we heard the sirens.

Chapter 17: Baton Rouge

In April 2002, we arrived in Baton Rouge, LA where we had been three times previously. We went directly to John's cousin's house. She worked for campus security at a nearby university. We stayed at the house for two days, both nights they had long discussions. Regarding these discussions, John told me once and only once, "If you needed to know, I would tell you." I didn't ask any questions. He explained on the third day of his reason for coming to Louisiana. We stole a car and cased another "target" (as he labeled human beings). Soon we figured out the guy's routine and we set up shop in an abandoned house about a hundred yards from the mall parking lot where the "victim to be" was parked. He enters the mall. I walk up to his car and puncture his tire. Shortly thereafter our target exits the mall; Muhammad lays there for a full ten minutes, but no shot. Something must be amiss, but what could it be, nobody has spotted us. Then John says, "He's all yours!" I replied, "You had a clear shot, the mall has cameras. While there is no security driving around, there is possibly millions of witnesses. "This is stupid." John's face never changed. I am in a total fit. "Are you finished?" he says. "Good, that is why you have to do it." (John makes a shape resembling my mouth chattering).

"You still feel this is wrong? I will not put up with this every time you need to complete a task." He peers through his binoculars. "Here he (the target) comes. He will be making at least three trips, as he has five carts. Well, you have fifteen minutes and only fifteen minutes. If he is still standing in 15 minutes, don't come to the restaurant." He walks off, heading to the car without looking back.

I checked my belt but he had both radios with him. Thinking to myself, "This is stupid, look at the size of the parking lot." I trot to the lot since he is making his last trip. "I won't make it, he is packing up, and he's leaving, shit!" "No he isn't, the engine is off." The target exits the truck, looks at his flat tire and swears. I am about twenty feet away.

He gets his tool box, tire iron, and begins to work on the bolts. He is paying me no attention. I must get him to the left side of the vehicle, at least then it will conceal him when he falls. I sit on the bumper, he feels the weight. I must get him to the left side. He then rises from his seat. He asks, "What do you want?" I walk to the left side to draw him over. I stare at him, still not responding, he picks up the tire iron. I walk as if trying to circle the truck; he counters, and comes to the left. He slaps the tire iron in his hand, I back away quickly. He slows his pace, we look at each other in the eye, he charges, about to swing, I duck and reach for my weapon in the holster which is located in the small of my back. He is shot in the chest. Mind you, this all happened in about 10 seconds. I walked away slowly while checking the time. I used the watch as a mirror. A truck is driving out; they are going to spot him. I crossed the street quickly. I try to quiet the sirens going off in my head.

I am now in full stride running behind the restaurants and businesses. Most of them, except the restaurants are closed as it is a small town. I reach the restaurant alongside the highway. Rummaging through the trash, I find a plastic bag and change my clothes. I remove my sweater and jeans. I am now dressed in a t-shirt and shorts. I enter the restaurant, but I am worried. There is no John in sight and his car is not in the parking lot. I grow more anxious by the minute. A few minutes later he pulls up. He squeezes me on the shoulder, calls the waitress. I hear the reeling of sirens, "Are you hungry?" "Yes, sir." I replied blandly. I whisper across the table, "Let's go!" John calmly says, "But you are hungry. I will take the blueberry pancakes." John says to the waitress, I then reply "I will have the same." He eats while I keep my head close to my plate. Thinking to myself, "What if someone walks in, I cannot wait for him to finish." I couldn't stand the pressure any longer and head for the car.

A few minutes later he joined me. He began slowly, "You were bent over him, why didn't you finish him behind the ear like I taught you? What were you doing?" I opened the plastic bag and handed him the man's wallet. He just shook his head and hands it back to me.

We returned to Baton Rouge after a few hours of having my ass chewed out for being sloppy. He ditches the car in a vacant lot and we are on the road by 11:00pm that night. "Six more states to Washington, on the way up you will perfect it." John said.

I sighed. Once again I didn't live up to his expectations. Being chided by him affected me. I cannot explain it, it's like my mission in life was to win approval in his eye, to be exactly like him. We moved up the West Coast, Texas, Arizona, New Mexico, Wyoming, Utah, Idaho, and Washington. We committed a few robberies along the way and up until the middle of May 2002.

Chapter 18: I See Death Calling

At the end of May 2002, Muhammad informs me that he has found his children. He believed that they were living on the East Coast, probably in the Maryland or D.C. area. John decided that we should spend the next few weeks making and testing silencers for the .308. While doing this, we lodge with Holmes, an old Army buddy of Muhammad's. Holmes' automotive repair shop had all the equipment we needed to make the silencer. We purchased all the components and assembled one of the two designs we were testing. In mid-June we *lost* the .308 and the silencer. During the preceding weeks we had cased a very prominent nightclub. The owner dropped off the money at a drop box at a bank across town in Tacoma, WA. Across the road from the bank were a small apartment complex and an abandoned parking lot covered with overgrown berry bushes, perfect for concealment late at night.

We decided to carry out the robbery on Friday night. Several cars were parked in the abandoned lot. As the night wore on the traffic in and out of the lot increased. Someone was holding a party in the neighboring complex. Over the radio Muhammad told me he could smell the liquor. I was stationed under a bench on the bank premises. Several small trees provided darkness because a few days earlier I had disabled the light closest to this bench. An hour before the target arrived some drunken kid ran over the rifle which got bent between the spokes of his rims. Muhammad had the rifle resting on its bipod and got up to relieve himself. During that time the four young men entered the lot and got into a truck. I guess the driver had to be drunk because instead of putting the truck in drive or first gear, he put it in reverse and ran over the rifle - the barrel of which got jammed in the spokes of his wheel. I witnessed the entire thing. When the young men exited the truck I heard them talking loudly about the rifle stuck in the left rear wheel and that they should call the cops.

We stole an AR-15 from the Bulls Eye Gun Store in Tacoma, WA three days earlier. I suggested that we take three days to make a silencer but Muhammad had disagreed.

We went to Olympia, WA to visit a friend of John's to pick up ID's, the black bag that contained money and Canadian passports for John, myself and his three children, along with all the money that John had saved from robberies and assassinations up to that point.

We were on the trolley in Seattle, WA when I felt my mother's presence. I nudged Muhammad, "My mother is here, I can feel it." Seconds later, I hear my mother's voice; she grabs my arm and walks to the front of the trolley, demanding that the driver stop the trolley. We're still in the station mind you and I see Muhammad exit the trolley from the rear as my mother and I exited the front. Muhammad walks toward the exit without looking over his shoulder once.

I have never seen my mother so scared, she is as tough as they come. I looked at Muhammad leaving and gave my mother a look that froze her in fear. She released my arm and staggered back a few paces. I ran in Muhammad's direction. Toward the exit behind me I could hear my mother in a half-sob, half-plead, "Lee, today you have run away from your mother and surely to your death!"

When I reached the top of the steps, Muhammad was waiting; I paused and turned to look at my mother one last time. In a split second, two images materialized and with them the emotions they evoked. The first image was of my mother through the open of the door throwing at me the makeshift rope of braided sheets I had attempted to hang myself with. She said to me, "Go ahead and kill yourself – do it – it's cheaper for me to pay for your coffin than it is to take care of you. So go ahead, kill your fucking self." The second image was of me taking my mother to see the school psychologist, the guidance counselor, and my vice-principal – in the immediate aftermath of the attempted suicide. The vice-principal explained to her why I needed her to stay in Jamaica. My mother cut the vice-principal off abruptly, stood up and walked out of his office. I grabbed her shoulder as she was exiting and said, "Can't you see you are losing me?" She removed my hand from her shoulder and looked at me as if I were the plague.

"Son!" Muhammad's voices called me back from my reminiscing reverie, "I am as dead to you now as I can ever be," were the words that stuck with me. My mother was the last thread on which tethered my precarious old-self. That cord had been snapped, all ties had been severed. I was a dead man walking in more ways than one.

It was back to the Greyhound bus heading slowly south. We arrived in Baton Rouge, LA. I breathed a sigh of relief, Muhammad's instructions were simple, "Don't say too much, you are here to observe and to take a much needed rest. This place is the epitome of a pitiful existence." We lodged with Muhammad's younger brother Edward, his wife, and their two teenage children Edward Jr. and Latoria. I am introduced as Muhammad's son.

After three days or so I could be found at the Tezano's place. I spent the days horsing around, cracking jokes and just being a teenager. The Tezano's lived up the street from Edward Senior. Muhammad and Edward grew up with Mr. and Mrs. Tezano; they were all in the same age group.

In my mind, all that remains is to find the children, do some surveillance, return to Washington State, and then on to Canada. Once in Vancouver, John had intended to lease or rent a house, open a business, resettle the children and enroll me in flight school. We already possessed what we needed as far as documents and identification, all of them were legitimate.

I pretended that everything was alright and that I was just a normal teenager. I got introduced by Muhammad to his two other sons, Travis, who was around twenty-three and a younger son (whose name I cannot remember).

Into the second week one Sunday afternoon I found John lounging in a lawn chair under the front yard at Edward's. Upon first meeting John, once we got close, he had instructed me on the meaning of over a dozen looks. I knew what the look he was giving me meant, he rose and walked across the street to a wooded area about twenty feet lower than the level of the street. I followed. John sat on a fallen tree, I sat beside him. He is staring at something in the distance not anything in the surroundings, his vision is more indrawn. He lapses into his monotone voice, a very clear and calm voice. He then explained that he intended to get back at America, by killing 25 people a week for four weeks that he wanted to use two snipers with silencers, which was easy enough. Even though we didn't have the silencers, we proceeded with the plan.

This is way – way out there - never had he even mentioned this plan. I protested, "Dad, I thought we were simply doing what was needed to earn money, find the children, get settled, return for the children and resume our normal lives in Canada, what happened to this plan?" John said, "The plan is to terrorize the Maryland, Virginia and D.C. metropolitan areas for four weeks, killing 100-200 people in the process. In phase two, we would use explosives for the next four weeks to up the ante." He then explained the exact model of an old police car we need to use as a firing platform and to use a technique that the IRA (Irish Republican Army) had implemented. To end the entire thing, we would kill one police officer in Baltimore, MD and decapitate him in a brutal manner. Everyone was going to attend his funeral, half the police force, the mayor, members of the city council, possibly even the governor. For maximum effect, we would plant our explosives, set with nails and ball bearings at the cemetery. With the use of both primary and secondary devices we would literally wipe out the police force. Once emergency crews responded to the scene, we would blow up the secondary devices. His eyes gleaned with rage that I had never seen before. Once this was all completed, we would then demand $10 million dollars.

John talked further of his plan, "The ten million dollars would be deposited in an overseas account. They will have two choices, a few hundred dead bodies or $10 million dollars. No tourism, no Christmas and we will shut down their money. The money we get will be used to train and school young black children like you, who never had a chance. Realistically, we will never be able to withdraw all the money at once, not even a quarter of that amount, but a million dollars will be enough."

"We're going to fuck with the only thing these people give a fuck about – *their money*. Everything along the entire Eastern Seaboard will be disrupted. Tourism, the holidays, all will come to a screeching halt. Because we do not have a silencer and we will be shooting out of the car, reasonably it must be five people per day; five is the golden mean – more but no less than five."

I asked, "Sir, it has always been your benchmark that one always sticks with the plan, never deviating. Why this sudden change? What does this have to do with getting the children?" "Son, I have a debt to pay. One stone used to kill three birds. I will terrorize the real terrorists! Secondly, I get my children back. Lastly, we will affect their bottom line where it hurts all in one swoop, and possibly get paid for doing so!" was his answer.

For the remainder of the day I am in shock. I know this plan cannot succeed without me. I cannot eat. I cannot think straight. I am at Edward's trailer, alone, sobbing. I write a suicide note and put a round in the .357 revolver, spinning the chamber. I squat in the corner of the bathroom, the pain of trying to hold in the sobs wrack my body with heavy tremors. Repeating to myself, "Lee you are going to die." I am balled up in the corner, my head and face between my knees. I am crying, "Lee, kill yourself. No! No! Not yet! Why don't you kill him?" I see Muhammad's face and picture his scornful face laughing at me and saying, "You kill me? Ha! Go ahead. Let me see you pull the trigger." I did not have the guts to do it.

"Run away? Fuck that!" I pulled the trigger, *click!* "I have $157.30 on me, this pistol, and some clothes. How will I live? Who do I turn to? What do I do?" *Click!* I pulled the trigger for the second time. I cock the hammer. "Lee, today you run from your mother, assuredly, you run to your death!" I recall my mother's last words to me, *click!*

"Lee, are you in there?" It was Edward Jr. "Yeah!" I replied, my voice breaking. "I need to take a leak." he said. "Look Ed, I have a bad stomach, just hold on a second." I smelled blood and looked in the mirror, shit my nose was bleeding. I cleaned the floor with some napkins. Edward is banging on the door. "Alright man." I said, "I am coming, damn!" I shouted.

I placed the .357 in the small of my back. I exited the bathroom; Edward squeezes past me and closes the bathroom door behind him. When I passed him I had used my hands to cover my face, pretending that I was wiping it with a napkin.

I moved the curtain, "Shit, John is coming." I needed to leave my suicide note where Latoria could find it. I hid in the bed under the sheets hoping that John will think I am asleep. John ducks in to check up on me, he closes the door. I decided to wait until Edward Jr. was done in the bathroom. Once Edward left, I used the glow from the streetlight to begin writing my suicide letter. Suddenly Ed Jr. entered the room and catches me. "Lee, you alright?" "I will tell John you aren't, he asked me to check on you." I jump quickly out of the bed and grab Edward's shoulder, "No, No! It is just my stomach aching, that's all. I just took some meds; I will be fine by tomorrow."

The next morning I call Edward Jr. into the room and closed the door behind him. I hand him the letter for Latoria. "Give this to Latoria once we leave. Ed – do not read it! Promise me – Ed!" He gives me his word.

"Lee!" yelled John. "Yes, sir," I responded, "I'm ready."

Chapter 19: The Walls Come Tumbling Down

The ride east was short and direct, we went directly to Clinton, Maryland. Wherever we went we did robberies. In Clinton, I robbed a small eatery. The remainder of the time was spent doing surveillance on Mildred Muhammad, the comings and goings of her friends, and learning the children's daily routine. Once this was done we moved on.

We went to Camden, New Jersey in August 2002 where we stayed with some of John's friends. While we were in Camden, John purchased a Chevy Caprice, which was essentially an old police cruiser. On the way south (where we left the AR-15 in a duffel bag with the explosives) is when John modified the car.

We added solar panels to the dashboard so I could run the laptop without draining the car's battery. Work was also done on the engine, making it more powerful. But the most important changes were made to the trunk of the car.

We removed the frame to separate the trunk of the car up from the inside. This alteration allowed either one of us to enter the trunk without being seen either before or after a shooting took place. All of the windows were darkly tinted.

The trek to and from Baton Rouge was a trail of bloodshed. We did robberies in Alabama, Louisiana and Georgia, all the way up the East Coast and into Maryland. In these robberies no one was fatally wounded.

In the final two weeks of September 2002, the idea was to spread sheer terror. Although Raleigh, North Carolina was our home base (This is where Muhammad had left the explosives and the other components for Phase II), we rode up and down the eastern seaboard doing numerous crimes and shootings. Once we had located the perfect areas to conduct the shootings and conduct phase two with the explosives, all that remained was to implement each step. My job was to be John's eyes and ears and to know each area inside out.

The number John had set to kill was 5 people every day for one month. This number was necessary for the "shock effect" that John had wanted. Everything went as planned until the eighth shooting where I broke down. During this four-day period of inactivity, John had wanted me to shoot a pregnant woman. I took all the shots that were taken outside the car and John took all the shots from inside the car. The problem is that I went out to take the shot two nights in a row, I didn't. I couldn't pull the trigger. I didn't want to do it. The whole purpose was to terrorize, so the decision to murder a pregnant woman was aimed to outrage and terrorize. I had the opportunity, but I couldn't do it. I broke down during this period and Muhammad ostracized me for my cowardice. I felt trapped. John asked me if I wanted to split the proceeds we had saved from all the robberies and gun selling but I told him "no." He kicked me out of the car.

I sat on the curb with $200.00 in my pocket and a duffel bag with a few items of clothing. I was in a total state of emotional paralysis. Several hours later John returned. I could not function outside of Muhammad's presence, meaning John was the brain and I was his "instrument" as he often referred to me. I didn't have to think. He would tell me what to eat, how to eat, and when to eat. I trusted John completely - he was consistent. Emotionally, I was completely dependent upon him.

I rested my head in my lap as I sat on the curb. I heard a vehicle stop before me and I looked up. The passenger door was open and John was smiling down at me. "Are you ready?" he asked. I said, "Yes, sir!" From then on, to my arrest, I was almost what he wanted me to be. John was still upset that we didn't meet the quota of killing five people per day.

Now, during this entire period we still did other activities including going to the cinema, gym and restaurants. The final shot, the Conrad Johnson shooting, was a failure from John's perspective. I had panicked and left the weapon behind. I had prepared for such a situation and hid the weapon in a drain pipe. Once the police had concluded their investigation I returned to the scene of the crime and retrieved the weapon. I swore that it was a trap, but the investigators had completely walked right by it.

We never really listened to the radio or watched the news, so we had no idea that an APB was out for our arrest. John broke a cardinal rule, he decided in the middle of the shootings to contact the police by leaving notes at the scene of several crimes. This was an impulsive decision that was never a part of the plan.

John decided to do one more shooting and then return to Raleigh, North Carolina to get the materials to begin the next phase; we had already selected the targets. Before the violence could escalate into the bombings, I fell asleep in the car when I was supposed to be on "watch."

The arrest was over in the time it takes to blink. John and I were immediately separated. I blamed myself for our capture for at least a year after our arrest. I did a lot of reckless things in the period leading up to my trial. I was a goner, I just didn't care. That was until fate intervened and a social worker who was appointed to assist me. Her help, along with the members of my legal defense team, saw some good in me worth salvaging. I couldn't see it in myself.

Chapter 20: Testifying Against Muhammad

For years I was trapped in a prison of shame, regret, blame and guilt. It was in the midst of this hellish state that I was extradited to Montgomery County, Maryland. While in Montgomery County Jail my meltdown worsened. However, I suffered in silence. I didn't lash out, act out or hurt myself. I tried to face each demon one-by-one. I wore a pleasant mask.

It was during this time that I realized that I was alone. No one had been with me in the midst of those emotions or in the turmoil that writhed agonizingly through every facet and aspect of my being. I came to grips with my addiction to rage. I recognized that responsibility and happiness are inextricably related. I realized that I could change, that presently each moment is neutral. Where I direct my attention dictates my experience. I saw the hidden fear behind my passive aggressive tendencies.

The constant presence of my social worker and the staff at CVA said volumes and helped me to stay anchored to reality beyond the world I habited between my ears. I was very angry. I had trusted John Muhammad with my life. I had revealed to him my hopes, fears and dreams and he used this knowledge against me, to manipulate me to his ends.

One day I was reading an article in the Washington Post and came across a story about Muhammad. I decided that I had to confront him. The only way to deal with pain is to accept it, own and confront it; any attempt to flee from pain is a futile effort. In doing so, I would only condemn myself to the fate of suffering ten-fold that which only had to be accepted, faced and endured but once.

I had learned that life has two roads, the right way and the right way. It may take years, lifetimes but one must reap as he has sown in the field of this body. The easy way out is always the hardest and longest route. In the same way that natural laws govern the physical universe, I was discovering that the same laws govern the inner life of man. The laws are unchanging, they don't fail us, we fail them through disobedience.

I wrote the prosecutor on Muhammad's case that evening and informed her of my willingness to testify against him. A meeting between me and the attorneys that represented me and the commonwealth took place two days later. I was told in no uncertain terms that I would receive nothing in exchange for my testimony.

The FBI used the opportunities of the protracted interviews to clear up several issues. I answered all questions truthfully, but without straying into too many crimes that the authorities were unaware of at the time. My psyche was very fragile. I left most of the unsolved incidents for later. I decided to gradually face each aspect of the process step-by-step. I had little help; I was my own priest, therapist, counselor, confidant, friend and enemy.

I was the prosecution's final witness. I described in detail the murders in Montgomery County and accepted my role as an accomplice. I was not afraid of Muhammad. I wasn't afraid of the cynicism and scrutiny or ostracism of the public. The desire for truth is itself the light, I too was coming to grasp – if even barely - attempting to understand, why.

Muhammad's cold stares simply cemented my resolve. I looked at him directly in his eyes. His once overpowering spell had long been broken. His words and charisma held no sway over my mind.

When it came time for Muhammad to cross-examine me, his first and seemingly only agenda was to reestablish his superiority over me by calling me "son." He refused to use my real name. I appealed to the judge, "Will you please direct the defendant to use my name your honor!" On and off he would try this tactic, each time he did I would not answer. I simply looked to the judge for guidance. Finally John abandoned this tactic.

He revisited our shared experiences in Antigua, first pointing out how he had accepted me into his family, into his home, how he taught me, took care of me – as if to say that I had betrayed him. So one-pointed was his intention to prove to himself that my mind still belonged to him that he neglected the more pressing and pertinent issues he could have addressed in his cross-examination.

I went from feeling hatred, to feeling pathetic – this man isn't my intellectual equal – what did I see in him? I was duped by this man? I could now see through his tactics, I recalled exactly how he used them and explained as best as I could when a question gave me an opening to elaborate on his blatant lies he had spun with his forked tongue.

I recalled the five nervous breakdowns I witnessed Muhammad have. He had become what he had so much warned me never to be, he had lied so much to himself; that he began to believe his own tales. He was caught in the madness of his own fabricated delusions. He was a goner, a mere carcass of the man I once idolized and respected. I felt pity.

At the end of my pleading to five to six counts of capital murder, the victims' families had a chance to speak. This was the most emotionally trying and painful memory of my life. But compassion, strange and mysterious as it can be, came in the guise of pain. I was a witness to Ahimsa (non-violence) on a level I didn't then comprehend.

Conrad Johnson's mother (the last victim to die) locked eyes with me and spoke from a place of depth and certainty of forgiveness that couldn't fail to pierce my heart like a thousand nails. It was genuine this gift, without demanding anything in return. By forgiving me, she had opened the door for me to forgive myself, albeit gradually, little by little, layer by layer. I shall never forget her.

My testimony for a time didn't resolve my mental anguish, on the contrary, the physical symptoms got worse, though I hid it well. I have witnessed and been an instrument of great atrocities; still many people have given the gift of kindness to me, when all I had to give in return was pain. "Hurting people, hurt people." The moment I realized that I no longer had to choose the role of the victim, that being an adult – now – I would no longer blame anyone. I have free-will. I have a mind.

This is the happiest I have ever been as I sit here. I can speak freely about my actions. I feel remorse, most definitely, but no longer am I enslaved by guilt. I do not hate myself. Now, is the only time, the only space and place I can live the life of my dreams.

Having lost all I desired of life, I went in search of value. I have and am learning to turn within, how to take my mind to my heart. I have found a reliable guide, one who can open the wonders of the inner worlds. I am equal to my circumstances. I have failed plenty, I even reached a point where I gave up, I have given my best – and they had failed me. Suffering is a fortunate thing in this world. Without it, our eyes wouldn't be inward turning; no awakening to a deeper yearning. I am enrolled in the University of Love.

No matter how haphazardly we search in everyone, everything, and everywhere else outside ourselves; no matter how blind or ignorant we may be – we are all seeking love. In being spurned by everyone else, I discovered what love is not. Everyone played their part. I could be stuck as a bitter, enraged human being, filled with self-hatred, but I am not.

The University of Love

Chapter 21: The Many Guises of Compassion

My first year in Red Onion State Prison was fairly quiet. I was housed in total segregation. Being confined to a prison cell 23.5 hours a day, I came face-to-face with my thoughts and images and the emotions they evoked. Admittedly, I no longer wanted to flee from or suppress the pain I had encountered. I had to face my pain in order to understand who, what, where, why and how I created my own circumstances. I realized that we all play a paramount and creative role in the circumstances in which we find ourselves. But how?

The impetus to begin the process of self-examination came through the work of a source, a person whom I was not fond of at the time. His name was Dr. Smith. Before being assigned to my case as the Commonwealth's mental health expert, Dr. Smith had made clear his views and had arrived at a verdict as to my guilt, and this was posted on the Internet. My attorney, Mr. Arif, tried to present the aforementioned printed views of Dr. Smith as evidence of bias, but the judge would not allow it. I recalled the 10-hour interrogation in which Dr. Smith rephrased the same question and asked it over and over again.

Anyhow, the program created by Dr. Smith was being aired on a local school channel back then. I watched each part of the series and it was a shock to my system. The process began to stir up the muck and debris of my past, and it was physically painful. I suffered severe flashbacks, recurring images that induced panic attacks, nose bleeds, black outs, migraines, chronic insomnia and I actually feared going to sleep.

In one episode of the series on the after-effects of crimes, Dr. Smith asked one of the participating prisoners, one by one, who was affected by your actions and by your crime? Time and again the answers would have a bordered focus circumscribed only to the prisoner, his thoughts of the immediate victims. I recall one instance where Dr. Smith took a prisoner charged with robbery and explained how his acts affected the victim's family, her neighbors and the community. This one criminal act had brought harm to so many people. As the list of affected parties grew in number, the psychological distance, and with it the barriers that I had created dissolved, gradually one by one.

I listed all the crimes I had participated in. There were over one-hundred and fifty such incidents ranging from petty theft, fraud, robbery, murder and terrorism. When I finished the list, I experienced my first panic attack. As I attempted a list of all persons affected, I blacked out, as if the meltdown caused an overload. I awoke to find myself caked with dried blood that was the result of a nose bleed. After the first panic attack, I had recurring dream of a little boy standing at a window, he had a glove and a baseball, and he was waiting for his father. Day after day he waited. While he never spoke, his thoughts were amplified, I could hear them. He would always turn to me, his eyes stained with all the full spectrum of pain and anguish. He would ask me, "Why?" "Why did you kill my father?" One by one, whether I was asleep or awake the images of the people I had murdered would haunt me. Two images in particular would surface before each recurring panic attack, the face of Conrad Johnson (the last person to be gunned down in what came to be known as the "D. C. Sniper shootings") and the eyes of Linda

Franklin's husband (The FBI analyst who was murdered at the Home Depot parking lot in Fairfax, Virginia).

The head psychologist at Red Onion State Prison at the time made it clear that he hated my guts. While I understood his reaction, I recognized that he could never help me, he could not be objective. Most of the psychologists I have come across during my time in prison are extremely cold, numb and distant. They are unable to connect with prisoners. They cannot really help. Plus, anything a prisoner reports will be used against him. It isn't safe to be honest.

I returned to an old and proven method to get a grasp over my mind and to get in touch with my feelings, so I started keeping a journal. I had kept a journal from the age of 8 to 15 before abandoning it for some reason. I had to write, I was compelled to write. I had to get it all out of my system. I attempted to dissect my life, to examine the actions, factors, environment and my reactions to see how I was led to or created the hell in which I was now a resident.

Malvo's cell - where he will spend the rest of his life

Lee's illustration of Muhammad's control (hand around his body)

2002-2010

Original Poetry by Lee Boyd Malvo

I Struggle with My Own Suffering

Mother I am angry
Father I am mad
Every time I think…
Every time I look at you
I grow sad.

I have struggled with suffering
In silence.

I have struggled with being
Invisible and alienated.
The pain accumulated
As unresolved frustration.

Many nights
Thoughts of suicide
Held me hostage.

For hours in the tormented Hell
Trapped behind my eyes,
Death and I negotiated.

From this nightmare I awoke
Released on the installment plan,
Paroled at dusk.

I struggle with rage
And the unintended consequences,
That still linger.
The hate I feel at times
When I look at my reflection.

I have struggled,
And continue
To struggle with my own suffering.

I feel the slap of rebuke
The sting of pain
-trial and error-
There are no excuses.

A Dying Breath

Some people see reason to rejoice
at the sight of a baby being born.
While I in my melancholy state
contemplate this and turn away,
seeing – in this miracle – cause enough to mourn.

Pain brought us into this world
a life of trial and error,
every joy is followed by sorrow
and suffering, is one guise or another,
awaits us all.

And, the curse,
the search,
for love and happiness,
this patient toil
of quiet desperation,
the sole pursuit
behind all our pursuits.
Pain is our life's companion.

I now see why
when a baby is born,
upon entering the world,
it cries with such tremendous depth,
for it has been re-introduced
to the agony of our mortal lot,
the anguish of dying breath.

The body is a corpse
waiting to happen.
Life is short and uncertain.
Death for all is certain,
swift and sudden.
O humankind – learn to – use this body well.

Aloneness

If it were not for suffering
our eye would never be
inward turning,
there would be no cause
for soul searching,
and life would be devoid
of those insights
that provide us with purpose
and that give life meaning.

All that I have found,
I have lost,
and with the spent days
of my life
I have paid the cost.

With this mind,
I long ago
began to draw
the blueprint
for this cell
-this Hell-
well made by my own mind.
This self-imposed prison.

With these hands
I did the deeds,
laying the bricks,
caught up in my own madness.

With my feet
I took all the steps,
all those miles that add up
to the present.

Aloneness (continued)

So, with each day,
with each feeling,
my attitude created my approach,
my approach molded in turn,
my experience.
I was building a house.
in which to live,
I was becoming
a character in the making.

Another cannot breathe for me.
So, where did I get off thinking
another should think and
could live for me?

No living thing can evade
the responsibility
for its welfare.

I have come face to face
with the ugly truth,
my greatest fear: aloneness.

I was afraid
very afraid
of being alone.

I –am – alone.
I am alone
in my joy
and in my pain.

I alone experience
the images, the elations,
joy, fantasies, vile affections and fear.

Aloneness (continued)

The inner reality
In-that very singular consciousness –
I am alone.

I am alone
when my secret life,
my secret lies, haunt me,

and when my conscience moralizes
and convicts me,
no one knows but I!

I will not decry my suffering,
for it is part in the parcel of life,
in my process of becoming,
a character in the making,
this inner house.

I am daily creating.
I get what I am,
so to speak.

For to not know sadness,
how could I then recognize,
much less appreciate happiness.

The sooner I accept sole responsibility,
and let go of the blame,
guilt, shame and regret,
the sooner I will stop
living in the past,
and at least, begin in part
to wrest myself
from its grasp.

<u>Aloneness (continued</u>)

I am the pivotal force
of either growth
or destruction
in my life,
no one else is responsible
for this choice.

It is dawning on me
albeit slowly,
that my mind,
creates my destiny.

Frankenstein

They taught me in school
much that is useful.
They equipped and instructed me
in the art of making a living.

So far, so good.
Though they forgot
in all their giving
to inculcate
how I am to live,
the need for moral instruction.

The imbalance in my psyche,
led me to believe falsely
that my worth
was solely dictated by
my achievements and possessions,
by the evidence of the objective
products in my mind.

Still, in the world
a deeper sense of meaning,
a deeper purpose,
was hard to find.

We are rarely driven by logic,
though we do flatter ourselves
to that we are indeed rational.

I would venture to say,
we are moved
by the force of our deepest sentiments.

I was a sailor
with a map
but no compass.
I was missing
that overarching framework

of ideals,
that would give the incongruous
nature of my values,
a more definitive form

All knowledge and no heart.
So many facts, so many tools,
and still, so little understanding.

Behold – Frankenstein –
a body devoid of soul.

Survival of Slavery

For too long
we have been surviving
There is a great difference
between survival and living.

Living,
is a baby's first smile,
when under its own power,
its own effort,
it smile in recognition
of its own joy,
in achieving understanding,
an inner experience
that cannot be taken away
or destroyed.

The entire purpose to
find meaning and substance
in its world
is happiness
and so it smiles.

This is the goal of life,
happiness,
its attainment and maintenance.

Now what happens to that child, when it realizes…
it cannot assert itself,
that is has no-self-to-assert,
what is it worth?

What does it say of a society,
a culture,
whose every framework of law
has a writing set in stone:
You-shall- not-pass!
Rule by force,
Rule by fear.

What happens when that child
realizes- that it had no family,
that its parents – jumping the broom
was a farce,
for they could not-protect-it?

That, in fact,
the entire course of their lives
was the maintenance
-of a fraud.

What happens
when it can no longer
lie to itself-
no longer pretend-
no longer from its mind
the truth suspend-
what does it do then?

Strive to attain
the unreachable
a life defined by others?
Existence-devoid-of
one moment
-one moment-of glory!

When suffering is mandatory
and black existence is purgatory.

Must the child then
castrate its mind
maintain restraint
and continue to suffer
without complaint?
The laws have changed
but still our children
wear the chains,
we have delivered them,
our sons and daughters,

into the straight jacket
of the system.

What do you say
to a world,
that places you in a corner
and tells you…
Give it up! Give it up!
Whatever-you do – give –up
-your soul!

Do you know
what it is
to kill a mind,
to clip its wings?

How do I reconcile this?
I close my eyes
clench and unclench
my fists.

How will I be remembered?
That I quit – gave up –
gave in, surrendered?
Until I can live,
I – must – survive.

<u>1864: Black Son</u>

Though not a coward
I could not move,
my mind was arrested
in the surrealness
of this one moment.

Standing, aghast,
bewildered by what
I had witnessed,
it took me some time
to recuperate,
to return to reality.

The course of the battle
the smoke,
the shouting charges
of the men in mud
up to their knees,
like pigs that squalor
for a foot of the land.

How can it be?
that humankind can be
so uncaring?

Is this what civilization
has become,
brother killing brother,
the father slaying his son?

What are the justifications
for such madness?
Slaves? Plantations?
Monetary enterprises?

The wanton bloodshed-
the wholesale slaughter
of men,

the destruction wrought
upon nature,
the price paid.

Awash in tears
then and now.

Ideas – yes – ideas
can move a mountain of men
to act contrary
to all reason.

The rapacious ideology
your life, years and labor
for the sake
of my pernicious gluttony,
in order to fatten
my pocket,
I am willing to
become a vulture -
scavenging the eyes
plucking them out
of another man's sockets.

The anxiety and anguish
rekindled, then wanes
as I again see his blood
and feel his pain.

I am sure I saw him
but I was afraid to be correct,
afraid to face such an eventuality.

How did I know he was there,
know exactly where to stare?

I saw the scream
and was wracked by the tremors
of his agony,
as the bayonet of reality

faced him in the mud,
being trodden on –
left to die.

Am I that last drop
that spilled from his eyes.
I shiver as I recall
his outcry.

My black brethren,
holding him in my arms,
seeing his wounds,
my sweat and tears
mingling with his sweat
tears, phlegm and blood.
There is nothing I could do
to save him
to staunch the outpouring
of his life.

It is impossible
to sum up what we shared
the things – the evil –
we had witnessed,
an enemy that could not
be killed
with my ammunition,
the battle for our psyche
the war of attrition.

Still in parting
he had an excellent expression,
tolls the bell
of freedom.

The Scent of Death

I was 5 years old,
walking to the bus stop,
just like any other school morning,
what I cannot forget
are those eyes –
that stared through me,
burning fear into
the parchment of my memory.

The police officer
came around the corner
and immediately a shot rang out.
His body sagged
and fell limp, just two feet from me.
Blood poured from a huge hole in his head,
death was instantaneous.

Two hands grabbed
and lifted my fear frozen body.
Behind the wall,
I found myself
looking up into his eyes
as they bored through me,
his index finger over his lips.

I heard the footsteps
from behind the wall
I could see the officers,
swearing, their faces went rigid,
they picked up their comrade.
I heard their footsteps, retreating around the corner.

He lifted me over a side wall,
that separated the adjacent yard
from the property where he took the shot.
He landed after each leap
with barely a sound,
he'd pause and stoop to listen,

there was no fear in his face,
he was completely composed.
Finally, after repeating this several times,
he placed me on a sidewalk
and pointed to the tenement yard
where I lived.

My last brush with death
was no less personal
only this time,
I was the armed assailant
evading the police.

Trapped behind the darkness
of my eyelids,
are horrific images
that used to haunt me,
they will not depart
from my memory,
the metallic scent,
of freshly spilled blood,
clings to me.

The Bullets are Tears

The bullets are tears,
we cannot relinquish
but through nightmarish means
we express our nightmares.

How many dreams alive died,
destroyed before my very eyes,
streams flowed from the cloudy skies
and dried on the shores of my cheeks,
as bitter salt?

How we remain victims
of the social oppression.
We carry open wounds,
the lingering fear
the debilitating apathy and despair
of history's whitest years.

I hear the bell…
for whom does death toll?
What's the difference between hell
and the place I've dwelled?

Whiff the reeking smell
of burnt brain cells
that dwell in cells.

The slaves new wage?
A new age?
The pavements – cry – red tears!

A Lie

A lie can only
continue to live on,
through a conscious choice,
                          to submit,
to the devices of our vices,
and these choices
create our destiny.

So, can you continue
to allow your weakness
to parade around
and make a fool out of you?

Conclusion

What you have just read reveals substantial evidence of a child who grew up emotionally absent. Lee's father, Leslie Malvo, was neglectful, committed adultery numerous times and did everything he could to divide the home. Leslie was forced out of the home because of these repeated infidelities. At a time in an adolescent's life when they need attention and stability the most, his father was not there for him.

Lee's mother, Una James, was emotionally, physically and psychologically (According to Lee Malvo, Una James suffers from bi-polar disorder) abusive towards her son. She scolded him unnecessarily, often hitting him with a belt until he was black and blue. Lee had even calculated a "beating formula," because he knew that failing to meet his mother's strict academic standards had its own repercussions. For every mistake that was made on his exams, three blows would occur. It seemed that these beatings were physical manifestations of Una's own struggles in dealing with life. Una spent more time contriving ideas and scheming family members and friends to care for Lee than trying to nurture him. Consequently, her numerous attempts to reach him on some emotional level always fell short.

Lee Boyd Malvo's childhood was, in a word, nightmarish. It was filled with seeing multiple deaths up close, including a relative, enduring repeated physical and sexual abuse, incest, neglect, psychological trauma, betrayal, abandonment and disappointment. Through all of this, Lee repeatedly mentioned his willingness to want to succeed. This became his coping mechanism. The grades he earned were a form of self-acknowledgement. "Making the grade" was the only positive thing he knew for sure in life.

Lee explained that he had to study very hard and that his SAT scores were average. He performed extra work in order to score another 100 pts. He tried his best, given that he had to adapt to at least ten moves before he reached the age of 15. By 16, he had been completely abandoned by both parents.

Left to live alone in Antigua, Lee made ends meet by dabbling in petty theft and other crimes, which was his foray into a life of crime and mischief. He also made the unfortunate mistake of befriending John Allen Muhammad, but this was no accident. While Lee had seen John and his son at a nearby electronics store in the past; it was actually his own mother who fully introduced John Allen Muhammad to her son.

The intention to meet the "American" (John Allen Muhammad) was purely at Una's request. It was actually her ulterior motive to illegally enter the United States that would cause the fateful meeting to occur on a far deeper level. This decision would be one that both mother and son would forever regret, and cost many lives in the process.

The difference between Una and John was that he offered an ear to Lee. He provided Lee with appreciation, encouragement and acknowledgment. John, whether contrived or genuine in his feelings, accepted Lee as his own son. John was the father-figure Lee had always been searching for, so he fully trusted him with his life, obeying his every word. He idolized him in almost every way possible. In fact, Lee admits often in his diary of being afraid of disappointing John. During an interview with Lee Boyd Malvo he admitted, "John was bad, he was terrible, but he was there!" In fact Lee's greatest fear was also his greatest motivator for John Muhammad to exploit - the fear of further abandonment.

Lee would do anything to keep what he knew of this relationship as long as it meant that love was returned. John provided Lee with the necessities in life and showed him new ways of thinking. While Lee's hopes were plausible, even justified, his belief that John would turn out to be the man he imagined was misplaced. What he sought was understanding and love; instead Lee Boyd Malvo's life amounted to following the dreams of a man whose personal agenda of retribution included terrorism, destruction and committing multiple murders across the country.

Surely many individuals have suffered similar childhood experiences where abuse, neglect and abandonment are all too common and have gone on to live normal lives. Others have come from broken homes and went on to lead a productive existence without embarking on a shooting rampage that ruined lives and families forever. While this may be true, those individuals probably were not abandoned by both parents at 15 years of age. Most importantly, they did not have a father-figure whose sole purpose was to make them into a soldier.

Lee shot various weapons at a gun range 9-10 hours a day. His every move was monitored both inside and outside the home.

Lee was trained to run five miles a day yet allowed only one meal. He was ordered to field dress weapons while blindfolded and convinced to disown his own birth mother. Lee would then be subjected to carefully edited speeches about black oppression and provided lessons on how to regain his lost black pride by committing murder all before being sent off to bed. Lee Boyd Malvo was different than most in many ways.

The options Lee faced once Phase I (the actual shootings) began were either death or to go along with a plan that would end his life anyway. John was three feet away from him at all times when they were driving, and he was always armed. Even on missions where Lee thought he was truly alone, John was right there, spying and judging his young protégé's every move.

John Allen Muhammad had a plan to get his children and head to Canada with Lee, but this plan did not fully begin until Lee's indoctrination into murder in February 2002. Muhammad's initial plan changed, and he was hell-bent on revenge and carnage with the goal of trying to get permanent custody of his children back from his former wife. John intended to kill every one of her (his ex-wife Mildred's) closest friends and associates to further ruin her life. All of this left very few options for a confused teenage boy who knew all too well the repercussions of failing to follow orders. Failure to follow John's orders would surely have resulted in Lee's own death.

Once Lee became involved in the first murder, even the slightest hesitation to fully carry out Muhammad's plan would have sealed his fate. At this crucial time period, there was no familial support for Lee Malvo since John had coerced Lee into choosing him over his own family. There were no other influences in his life besides John Allen Muhammad. It was all he knew.

Lee Boyd Malvo was convicted for two murders in Virginia on December 18, 2003. He pled guilty to an additional murder and an attempted murder charge in Virginia on October 26, 2004. Additionally, Lee pled guilty to six counts of murder in Maryland on October 10, 2006.

He will serve the rest of his life in Virginia without the possibility of parole. While admitting responsibility and remorse for his crimes, he has also forgiven himself for what he has done. This does not condone his actions, but without accepting self-forgiveness, Lee would never have allowed this private information to be released.

Lee has destroyed many lives and families. He does he shy away from admitting the magnitude of his actions and is profoundly aware that he has ruined his own life. Making the best of a windowless cell (the cell has a window, but Lee cannot see out of it) no bigger than a compact car's parking space, he passes the time by drawing or doing yoga. Like most inmates serving life sentences, he does not look too far into the future. The reason for this is self-preservation. Harping on a future of monotony, isolation and forced correctional facility routines for the next 5 decades is far too horrible for him to mentally comprehend.

Now, at 27 years old, he has spent nearly a decade in isolation. All that is left of his life is to think about what he has done. The size of his cell far surpasses the entrapment his mind creates, which is his true prison. Nightmares continue to haunt him, seeing the victims as they fall. Lee will never escape his choices, his deeds or the moniker, "The D.C. Sniper."

The purpose of this book was to provide unknown details and insight about Lee Boyd Malvo's mindset. This intimate diary shows the damaging effects that early-life trauma can have on certain individuals. When these triggers are enflamed by other negative factors or external influences, they can make certain individuals act out in highly unpredictable ways.

Anthony Meoli, MA, J.D.

Printed in Great Britain
by Amazon

33333673R00126